WICCA

WHEEL OF THE YEAR MAGIC

A Beginner's Guide to the Sabbats, with History, Symbolism, Celebration Ideas, and Dedicated Sabbat Spells

LISA CHAMBERLAIN

Wicca Wheel of the Year Magic

Copyright © 2017 by Lisa Chamberlain.

Published by **Chamberlain Publications (Wicca Shorts)**

ISBN: 1546669655

ISBN-13: 978-1546669654

Disclaimer

No part of this publication may be reproduced or transmitted in any form or by any means, mechanical or electronic, including photocopying or recording, or by any information storage and retrieval system, or transmitted by email without permission in writing from the publisher.

While all attempts have been made to verify the information provided in this publication, neither the author nor the publisher assumes any responsibility for errors, omissions, or contrary interpretations of the subject matter herein.

This book is for entertainment purposes only. The views expressed are those of the author alone, and should not be taken as expert instruction or commands. The reader is responsible for his or her own actions.

Adherence to all applicable laws and regulations, including international, federal, state, and local governing professional licensing, business practices, advertising, and all other aspects of doing business in the US, Canada, or any other jurisdiction is the sole responsibility of the purchaser or reader.

Neither the author nor the publisher assumes any responsibility or liability whatsoever on the behalf of the purchaser or reader of these materials.

Any perceived slight of any individual or organization is purely unintentional.

YOUR FREE GIFT

Thank you for adding this book to your Wiccan library! To show my appreciation, I'm giving away an exclusive, free eBook to my readers—*Wicca: Little Book of Spells*.

The book is ideal for anyone looking to try their hand at practicing magic. The ten beginner-friendly spells can help you to create a positive atmosphere within your home, protect yourself from negativity, and attract love, health, and prosperity.

You can download it by visiting:

www.wiccaliving.com/bonus

I hope you enjoy it!

LEARN ABOUT WICCA
ON THE GO

Want to learn about Wicca during your morning commute, or while doing your household chores? These days it can be difficult to find the time to sit down with a good book, which is why I'm thrilled to announce that all of my books are now available in audiobook format!

Best of all, you can **get the audiobook version of this book or any other book by Lisa Chamberlain for free** as part of a 30-day Audible trial. Members receive free audiobooks every month, as well as exclusive discounts. It's a great way to experiment and see if audiobook learning works for you.

If you're not satisfied, you can cancel anytime within the trial period. You won't be charged, and you can still keep your book!

To choose your free audiobook from over 20 books about Wicca and related topics, including best-sellers *Wicca for Beginners* and *Wicca Book of Spells*, simply visit:

www.wiccaliving.com/free-audiobook

Happy Listening!

CONTENTS

INTRODUCTION

If you're reading this guide, you probably already know that Wiccans celebrate several Sabbats, or holidays, over the course of a year. These eight holy days, spaced roughly six weeks apart, make up the Wiccan "Wheel of the Year," a term that emphasizes the ever-turning nature of life on Earth.

Of course, the Wheel of the Year is not unique to Wicca—many other modern Pagan spiritual paths also observe these ancient sacred days, oftentimes with traditions and customs similar to those found within Wicca. The information in this guide is rooted in Wicca, but much of it is applicable to Pagans of all stripes, as well as anyone who is simply curious about the rich traditions surrounding these milestones of the Old Religion.

It's important to note that Wiccans also observe twelve (sometimes thirteen) Esbats, or ritual observances of the Full Moon. These monthly Esbats are often referred to as "the second wheel of the year" and together with the Sabbats make up the full Wiccan religious calendar.

Because a guide of this length could never do justice to each celebration involved in the entire Wiccan year, our focus here will be on the Sabbats, which mark the Sun's journey around the Earth from season to season. This is not intended to dismiss the importance of the Esbats, but simply to allow for a more thorough exploration of the eight "days of power" and what they mean to those who honor them.

In Part One, we'll introduce the general concepts inherent to the Wheel of the Year, a brief history of its development within Gardnerian Wicca, and a framework for approaching the practice of magic as part of your Sabbat celebrations.

Part Two devotes a full chapter to each of the Sabbats: their significance within the context of the ever-changing seasons, the part they play in the mythological cycle of the Goddess and the God, and the spiritual themes they ask us to reflect upon as we celebrate them. You'll also learn about the historical origins of each holiday and the associated traditions and practices that have been handed down over the centuries from our European pagan ancestors.

Finally, you'll find magical correspondences for spellwork and celebration of each Sabbat, as well as spells and other magical workings tailored specifically for each point on the Wheel.

Whether you are just starting out in Wicca, or are a seasoned practitioner looking for new perspectives, may these pages support and inspire your journey.

Blessed Be.

PART ONE

THE WHEEL
AT A GLANCE

INVENTING
THE WHEEL

In the days before clocks and calendars, people marked the passing of time and the turning of the year by following the movements of the Sun and the stars. Their "months" didn't contain 30 or 31 measured days, but instead followed the cycling of the Moon from New to Full and back to New again.

It was Nature that told them what time it was, and our ancestors depended entirely on Nature's clock for their sustenance. A hard winter, a weak harvest or a decline in wild game could mean extreme misfortune and even death. So it's no surprise that they regularly took time to pay homage to Nature, in the form of their gods and goddesses, to express gratitude for their blessings and ask for assistance in the coming season.

The rituals and traditions used to mark the turning of the seasons in the ancient world varied widely across the globe and evolved over time. In the Western world, where Wicca finds its roots, there's a rich diversity of lore from the ancient Egyptians, Greeks, Romans, Celts and Germanic peoples. These cultures worshipped different gods and goddesses and had different names for their holy days, but the dates on which their observations took place were actually fairly consistent.

For example, in early February, the ancient Egyptians celebrated the Feast of Nut in honor of this mother goddess' birthday, while the Romans were busy with the purification and fertility rituals of Lupercalia, a holiday commemorating the mythical founders of Rome. The Celts also saw this as a time of purification as they celebrated Imbolc, and the Swedish Norse observed Disting, a time to honor the feminine spirits of the family. Weather divination was practiced in many cultures on this day, including among Germanic tribes, whose particular custom has survived all the way into the present in the U.S. "holiday" of Groundhog's Day.

Wicca was born out of a desire to reconnect with the spiritual practices of our ancestors—those who lived and worshipped in the old ways, before the Christianization of Europe (and much of the rest of the world). Inspired by the English occult revival of the late 1800s, Gerald Gardner and others set about reviving what they believed was an ancient pan-European religion, nearly wiped out by the Church but still surviving in hidden pockets of England and elsewhere.

An important aspect of the newly-reconstructed "witchcraft," as it was called by Gardner and his coveners, was the observing of the old pagan holidays, or "Sabbats" as they came to be known. These were the feasts and festivals that had long been coopted by the Christian Church in its efforts to stamp out the Old Religion once and for all. In addition to meeting at the Full Moon, Gardner's new 20th-century coven would meet on the occasions of these ancient festivals and enact special rituals to celebrate them.

Originally, Gardner's coven marked only the four cross-quarter days of November 1, February 2, May 1, and August 1. These dates were based on the ancient Celtic calendar, which divided the year into a "dark half," or Winter (from Nov 1st to

April 30th) and a "light half," or Summer (from May 1st to October 31st).

In this system, which was based on agricultural cycles, the dates of February 2 and August 1 mark the halfway points, or "cross quarters," of each half of the year. The coven would meet on the evening before the cross-quarter day, which is in line with the Celtic tradition of the new day beginning at sundown. Hence, these Sabbats as envisioned by Gardner were called "November Eve," "February Eve," and so on.

Other pioneers of the new Paganism during this time, such as the Order of Bards, Ovates and Druids, were incorporating additional ancient sacred dates into their practices. For millennia, the Summer and Winter Solstices were of the utmost importance to the Norse and Anglo-Saxon peoples, and many cultures in Mesopotamia and elsewhere observed the Spring and Autumn Equinoxes. Neolithic structures throughout Ireland and the UK suggest that these astronomical occasions were significant to the predecessors of the Celts as well.

Gardner ultimately added these solar holidays to the cross-quarter days, creating what we now know in Wicca as the eight-fold Wheel of the Year. As Wicca evolved and spread, the Sabbat days took on more specific names, usually borrowed from the ancient cultures that celebrated them.

These names vary across traditions, but the most common ones in use today are a blend of Celtic and Norse/Anglo-Saxon names: Yule, Imbolc, Ostara, Beltane, Litha, Lammas, Mabon and Samhain. Aidan Kelly, an influential figure in Wicca and other modern Paganism, is credited with coming up with this naming system in the late 20th century.

Of course, much has been learned since Gardner's day about the original theory of the ancient pan-European religion, or "witch-cult" as it was called—namely that there wasn't one.

It's true that many similarities can be found in ancient practices across wide swaths of Europe, due to the conquest of large territories by the Celts, the Romans, and the Germanic tribes. But each region still had its own distinct religious identity, making for a broad diversity of deities, beliefs, and customs. And there's scant evidence that any one ancient civilization in Europe marked all eight of the modern Sabbats.

Furthermore, the celebrations on these days would not have been only for the "witches" of the time—instead, entire communities participated in rituals and festivities. So people who believe that the Wiccan Wheel of the Year is a historically accurate revival of pre-Christian paganism are essentially incorrect.

Nonetheless, it could be argued that as the Wheel has evolved over the past several decades, via the expansion of Wicca and other modern Pagan belief systems, we now have something that comes closer to a "pan-European witch-cult revival" than Gardner could ever have envisioned. While the ritual component of Sabbat celebrations tends to be specific to Wicca—the honoring of the God and Goddess as viewed through a Wiccan framework—many practitioners also observe traditional customs that date back to antiquity.

For example, the ancient tree-worshipping practice now known as the Maypole is a popular way to celebrate Beltane, while those who work with magical herbs might make a point of gathering some at Litha, when herbs are traditionally thought to be at their most potent.

Indeed, the wide range of practices we see today—whether passed down through the generations or discovered by historians and anthropologists—provides eclectic Wiccans and other Pagans with increasingly more authentic information to choose from as they create their own Sabbat celebrations.

A TIMELESS CYCLE

The ancients lived by a fundamental truth that is often lost in our fast-paced world—that time is circular as much as it is linear.

The Celts understood this intrinsically, as you can see when examining just about any piece of Celtic artwork. The infinite looping of interweaving lines in the knots and crosses evokes a sense of creation without beginning or end. This same "loop" would have been experienced by all who observed the regularly shifting patterns of the Sun's journey across the sky, from its southernmost point at the Winter Solstice to its northernmost point at the Summer Solstice, and back again.

Following the Wheel of the Year helps us integrate this concept of circular time into our lives. As we mark each Sabbat we are consciously witnessing the turning of each season in exquisite detail, honoring the cycles of life and death, of growth and decay. It also helps us to be more often in the present moment, as the steady flow of holidays to prepare for and celebrate keeps us from rushing headlong through the seasons with barely a passing glance at the natural world.

Then there is the sense of rhythm that the Wheel provides— the equal increments of days and weeks between the Sabbats that help us anchor our sense of time passing in a beautiful symmetry. The eight-fold structure gives definition to a truth we've always subconsciously understood—that there are not four seasons but eight, as the "in-between" seasons bridge the gaps between the "cardinal" seasons of winter, spring, summer and autumn.

This cyclical quality is also seen in the dynamic relationship between the Goddess and the God. As the seasons turn, the divine pair shifts from mother and child to co-creative consorts and then back to mother and child.

Each year at the Winter Solstice, the Goddess gives birth to the God, and each spring she is restored to her Maiden aspect as the two grow together. As summer begins they unite as lovers and the God impregnates the Goddess, ensuring that he will be born again after his death in late autumn, when the Mother Goddess once again becomes the Crone.

Indeed, each deity is forever changing aspects—from young to old, from strong to weak and from bountiful to barren. And the non-linear quality of time is even further demonstrated in that both God and Goddess are manifest in more than one aspect at once: the Goddess is both Mother and Crone in the dark, cold months, and both Mother and Maiden in the early spring. The God is a seed in the Goddess' womb even as he ages and dies at the end of the growing season.

We honor these shifting roles and aspects throughout the year, with each Sabbat representing a point in the overarching story. This close participation with the cycles of the season is what some Wiccans refer to as "turning the Wheel."

NAMES AND ORIGINS

The eight Sabbats can be viewed as two interlocking sets of holidays: the cross-quarter days and the solar days.

In many traditions, a further distinction is made between the greater Sabbats and the lesser Sabbats. The cross-quarter days are called the greater Sabbats because they fall at the points where the shifts between seasons are most palpable, and these are considered to be days of strong power. They also happen to be the holidays we have the most detailed information about when it comes to ancient pagan customs, whether it's the Greeks, the Romans, or the Celts.

Many modern Wiccan practices on these days are rooted in what we know about the ancient Irish, who were able to keep much of their early literature safe from destruction during the Dark Ages. This may be why the cross-quarters take their names largely from the Irish traditions: Imbolc (February 2), Beltane (May 1), and Samhain (October 31). The exception here is Lammas (August 1), which is Anglo-Saxon in origin, but many Wiccans and other Pagans use the Irish name Lughnasa for this Sabbat.

Less is known about the specific details of the solstices and equinoxes, but what we do know is mostly rooted in ancient Norse and Anglo-Saxon cultures. The solstices in particular would have been celebrated by those living in the northern reaches of Europe, where the differences in daylight over the course of the year are more stark than elsewhere on the continent.

The names for these solar Sabbats are less historically accurate than the names of the cross-quarter days, with Yule (December 21) being the most traceable back to an actual pagan celebration on that date. The names Ostara (March 21) and Litha (June 21) are related to ancient Norse culture, but were not necessarily the names of holidays observed on those dates. Mabon (Sept 21) is the most "invented" of all the Sabbat names, taken from a Welsh mythological figure loosely related to the mother-son archetype of the Goddess and the God.

Again, these names do vary across Wiccan and other modern Pagan traditions. For example, people on the newly-evolving path of Norse Wicca may use Norse names for all of the Sabbats. Those who align more with the Celts might decline to use the standard names for the solar holidays and simply refer to them as "Summer Solstice," "Autumn Equinox," etc.

However, with all the diversity of names, customs, etc. to be found around the Wheel of the Year, there are usually a few things in common: feasting, ritual, and appreciation for the natural world in all of its beauty and abundance. And for those Wiccans who include spellwork in their practice, the energies surrounding the Sabbats make them excellent opportunities to work magic.

SABBAT MAGIC

Sabbats are known to many Wiccans as "days of power," since they occur at significant moments in the solar year—the solstices and the equinoxes—and at the cross-quarter points in between, when Earth energies are at their height. (Full Moons, or Esbats, are also days of power, but the focus there is on lunar energies.)

Witches often like to include spellwork and/or spellcraft (creating magical oils, incense, amulets, etc.) as part of their Sabbat celebrations. Of course, any type of magic worked with proper focus and intention will have some success no matter what day it is, but since you're already going to spend time at your altar on Sabbat days, you may as well harness the available extra power!

To maximize your magic's potential, it's useful to plan spellwork that aligns with the particular energies of each Sabbat. For example, take advantage of seasonal associations when it comes to choosing a magical goal.

Summer is traditionally a time for workings related to love, marriage, strength and energy, while winter is best suited to banishings, healing work, and magical and spiritual development. Spring is ideal for spellwork involving planting and outward-focused action, while autumn is a time for harvesting and turning our attention to inner work. You can also plan spells that align thematically with each Sabbat—for example, working for romantic goals at Beltane and banishing negative influences at Samhain.

Connecting with our pagan forbears through our actions on Sabbats is another way of strengthening any magical work we may undertake. For the ancients, most of these sacred occasions were fire festivals, honoring the Sun's role in sustaining life.

Bonfires, torches, and associated fire rituals played a central role in the celebrations, and some of these traditions are still practiced to this day. Fire is indeed a potent part of magic, representing light and transformation, and should be part of your Sabbat activities whether or not any spellwork is involved—even if it's in the form of just a few candles on your altar.

Another key component of Sabbat festivities that connects us to our ancestors is the act of preparing and enjoying a feast. The transformation of raw materials (vegetables, grains, animal flesh) into a delicious meal is its own kind of magical co-creation with the Universe. Even if you're celebrating as a solitary Wiccan, you can still incorporate "kitchen witchery" into your Sabbat meal by charging or blessing your food as you prepare it.

Of course, you don't have to work any spells on a Sabbat for the day itself to already be magical. In fact, there are Wiccans who don't practice magic at all, and their Sabbats are no less powerful and life-affirming than anyone else's.

Indeed, many different people from a wide range of Wiccan and other modern Pagan traditions are celebrating on these days, and the cumulative energy of these celebrations—past and present—contributes to the power already inherent in the Earth energies on these occasions.

So know that no matter how you choose to mark the Sabbats, you are participating in an ageless, timeless tradition of honoring Nature and the workings of the Universe, and your contributions are most welcome.

TURNING THE WHEEL

Now that you've been introduced to the origins and development of the Wheel of the Year as a whole, it's time to meet the individual Sabbats that comprise these eight days of power.

In Part Two, we'll take a close look at each of the greater and lesser Sabbats. You'll learn a bit about the historical contexts from which these modern holidays have evolved, and how these sacred days honor the co-creative relationship between the Goddess and the God.

You'll also find tips and ideas for holding your own Sabbat celebrations, and a few suggested spells and other magical workings that correspond with the themes and season of each holiday. So if you keep a Book of Shadows, you might want to grab it now, since you're bound to find information that will help you plan your next Sabbat!

PART TWO
THE SABBATS

OLD TRADITIONS MADE NEW

One of the key qualities of Wicca that has fueled its expansion over the past several decades is its dynamic capacity for reinvention and reinterpretation. There is a basic framework in place in terms of general beliefs and practices, but there's no universally agreed-upon way to go about any of the specifics, including Sabbat celebrations.

There are still lineage-based covens like those in the Gardnerian and Alexandrian traditions, whose members follow ritual protocols established early on in Wicca's development. But even these groups are bound to alter at least some details, as each coven is a unique collection of individuals with their own understanding of the original material. In fact, those familiar with the history of Wicca will recognize that even Gardner revised and reworked his own original Book of Shadows.

And as Wicca has grown and evolved, infinite variations on the older traditions have emerged. This is in large part due to eclectic practitioners, but it's also because creativity and invention are simply part of the experience of the Craft itself. In fact, many people who identify as Wiccans and Witches today feel perfectly comfortable improvising and inventing their rituals and other traditions around the Sabbats.

Therefore, you won't find any instructions about what to do or say during your formal Sabbat rituals in the following pages. (For those who would like help getting started with Wiccan ritual format, examples can be found in many sources in print and online.) Instead, the focus here is on getting a solid sense of what each holiday is all about, so you can begin developing your own approach to celebrating from a well-informed perspective.

In each chapter, we'll explore the seasonal context of the Sabbat and the associated themes that are often incorporated into Wiccan and other Pagan observances, including the stage it represents in the mythological cycle of the Goddess and God. We'll also take a brief tour of what is known of the pagan history behind each Sabbat—the myths, beliefs and customs that have inspired our modern celebrations—and common ways in which these have been incorporated.

PLANNING YOUR SABBAT

Of course, you'll also find suggestions for approaching your own Sabbat celebrations, whether you're a solitary practitioner or working with fellow Witches. Again, the possibilities here are infinite, and your choices will depend on your tradition (or lack thereof), your level of experience, and what each of these days means to you personally. That being said, there are two elements that most Sabbat celebrations have in common: the altar and the feast.

Setting up your altar for a Sabbat is a wonderful way to get into the spirit of the holiday. Whether you have a full-time altar or sacred space, or whether you're sprucing up an end table, it's hardly a Sabbat without special decorations—seasonal symbols, altar cloths, corresponding candles, flowers, herbs and crystals, etc. If you can, start setting up a day or two before the Sabbat, but if this isn't possible you can still start gathering the items you'll put on the altar when the time comes.

The altar is the focal point for your Sabbat ritual, so the more attention you put into it, the more receptive you will be in your connection with the God and Goddess. And it doesn't matter whether your altar is simple or elaborate—it's the energy with which you put it together that matters. You'll find detailed suggestions for altar decorations for each Sabbat under the "Correspondences" heading.

For solitary practitioners, a "feast" may be a little harder to pull off. But this word doesn't have to be taken literally. Whether you cook yourself a nice meal, or simply enjoy a healthy snack, just be sure to treat yourself to some nourishment from Nature at this time. Suggestions for seasonally appropriate foods are also included in the Correspondences in each chapter.

As for magic, you'll find two examples of spellwork in each chapter that are aligned with the seasonal and divine energies of the Sabbat. These can be followed as-is or adapted to suit your individual style. They can also be a springboard for more ideas about how to approach magical work on these days of power.

A NOTE ON DATES

The calendar dates given in this guide are the most commonly observed. However, the actual dates on which these holidays are observed can vary for a few reasons.

When it comes to the solar (or lesser) Sabbats, the exact moment of each solstice and equinox varies from year to year, due to a slight misalignment between the Gregorian calendar and the actual rate of the Earth's rotation around the Sun. For this reason, a range of dates is provided for these holidays.

For cross-quarter (or greater) Sabbats, some sources give the day before, in keeping with the Celtic tradition of the day beginning at sundown, so you will see both options in this guide.

Finally, for those living in the Southern Hemisphere, the dates of the Sabbats are completely reversed, so that Yule falls in June and Litha in December, and so on. These dates are also noted.

Some Wiccans, rather than following the modern calendar, use the movements of the Sun or the Moon to determine their cross-quarter day celebrations. A "cross-quarter" day is technically the astronomical halfway point between the two adjoining solar days—for example, Samhain marks the midpoint between the Autumn Equinox and the Winter Solstice.

The actual midpoint, however, usually occurs closer to November 6 or 7, so some covens and individuals may hold their Samhain celebrations then, instead of October 31st. Others may observe it on the first New Moon of the month, or of the first New Moon of the Zodiac sign in which the cross-quarter day falls.

Obviously, there's a lot of variance here from year to year, so these alternate dates are not cited in the guide, but that doesn't mean you can't follow one of these systems if it resonates with you.

No matter which date you celebrate your Sabbat, just be sure to approach it with joy and reverence for the natural world, the Goddess and God who create and sustain life, and the beauty of the cycle of life and death that keeps the Wheel forever turning.

YULE
(WINTER SOLSTICE)

Northern Hemisphere: December 20-23

Southern Hemisphere: June 20-22

Pronounced: Yool

Themes: rebirth, quiet introspection, new year, hope, setting intentions, celebration of light

Also known as: Winter Solstice, Midwinter, Alban Arthuan, Saturnalia, Yuletide

Celebrated on the date of the Winter Solstice, Yule is the point on the Wheel of the Year when we acknowledge the beginning of the return of the light. The nights have reached their longest point, creating a sense of darkness that is almost overbearing. The air is cold, the deciduous trees are completely bare, and for those in northern climates, the season of snow is in full swing.

Yet as far as the Sun is concerned, this is a turning point toward increased daylight, and the promise that warmth of the growing season will eventually return. The longest night will now be behind us, and the Sun will stay with us later each day, rising ever higher in the sky until the Summer Solstice, the turning point on the opposite side of the Wheel.

However, it will be a few weeks before this is noticeable, as the increase in daylight is only gradual at first. The Sun actually appears to not alter its path across the sky at all during the days around the Winter Solstice. In fact, the word "solstice" comes from a Latin phrase meaning "sun stands still."

Likewise, much of Nature seems to be still at this point. Birds have migrated south, many animals hibernate, and the snow covering the ground seems to have a quieting effect on the landscape. This is a time of turning inward, hunkering down, and tuning in to our deepest selves.

Many people see these short days and long nights as a time of self-reflection, spiritual study, and intention-setting for the coming year. But before the deep winter sets in, we gather with friends and family to celebrate the renewal of the Sun and the hope that comes with emerging from the darkness. This has always been a traditional time for both spiritual observance and merriment, and still is today, as we can see in the many different holidays and festivities associated with the start of the winter season.

In many Wiccan traditions, Yule is the start of the new year. The seasons of the Wheel, and the annual story of the God and the Goddess have completed the circle and now begin again.

The Goddess gives birth to the God, fulfilling the intention the divine pair set when they coupled at Beltane. As the Sun God, his symbolic death and return to the underworld at Samhain led to the darkness of the past six weeks, and now his rebirth brings back the light. The Goddess has transformed once again from her Crone aspect back to the Mother, who will now rest awhile from her labor and emerge rejuvenated in the spring.

This segment of the mythological cycle is at the heart of the Wiccan understanding of reincarnation—after death comes rebirth into new life. The Sun illustrates this truth through its cyclical disappearance and reappearance. The Earth, which never disappears, represents the never-ending presence of the divine Universe.

WINTER MAGIC
AND MERRIMENT

Of all the solar Sabbats, Yule is probably the one most clearly rooted in an ancient pagan holiday, as it takes its name from a festival held in Germanic and Scandinavian cultures around the time of the Solstice (though the original Yule likely lasted for several days).

Of course, many other peoples of the ancient world also observed the Winter Solstice, as we can see by the number of Neolithic monuments—like Newgrange in Ireland—built to align with the sunrise on this day. The Romans celebrated Saturnalia around this time, which involved feasting and exchanging gifts as well as ritual sacrifice. In Persia, this was when worshippers of the god Mithra celebrated his birth. And the Druids of the Celtic Isles are said to have gathered sacred mistletoe and sacrificed cattle on the solstice.

But while some forms of Wicca may base their Yule celebrations on some of these other regional traditions, in general the Norse and Anglo-Saxon customs that give the Sabbat its name are what the day is best known for.

In the lands of Northern Europe, the Solstice festivities were the last opportunity for most people to socialize before the deep winter snows kept them from being able to travel. Great gatherings were held by the Germanic tribes where feasting, drinking, and ritual sacrifice of livestock took place. Bonfires were lit and toasts were drunk to the Norse gods such as Odin and Thor.

These activities helped ensure a prosperous growing season in the coming new year, which was dawning now with the Sun's reemergence from the dark shadows. Some of the traditions observed during these ancient festivals—such as the Yule log, decorating with evergreen boughs and branches, warm alcoholic beverages known as wassail, and group singing—continued on through the centuries and are still part of many Christmas celebrations today.

The Yule log in particular was widespread in Europe, with many different regional customs attached to it. Traditionally made from a large log of oak, it was decorated with pine boughs, holly, or other evergreen branches and doused with cider or ale before being lit at the start of the festivities. In many places, this fire was lit with a piece of wood saved from the previous year's Yule log.

The log was supposed to be harvested from the land of the household, or else given as a gift—to purchase it was deemed unlucky. The Yule fire was tended so that it didn't burn out on its own, in part so that a piece of the log could be saved to start the following year's fire. The length of time for the fire to burn varied but was usually between 12 hours and 12 days.

The Yule festivities—caroling, games, the exchanging of gifts—took place around the warmth of the fire. In some places, the ashes from the Yule fire were used to make magical charms, sprinkled over the fields to encourage the crops, or tossed into wells to purify the water. As with so many other pagan festivals, we can see that the magical power of fire was alive and well at Yule!

The most obviously pagan remnant surviving in today's holiday traditions is probably the use of mistletoe. This parasitic plant (called so because it grows attached to a host plant, usually oak or apple trees) was significant to both the Norse and Celtic cultures, as well as the ancient Greeks and Romans. It's not clear why "kissing under the mistletoe" became a tradition, but it's thought to come from an ancient Norse myth involving the goddess Frigga and the death and restoration of her son Baldur.

The significance of mistletoe at the Winter Solstice likely comes from the Druids, who viewed the plant's ability to stay green while the oak it grew on was without leaves as a sign of its sacred powers. The mistletoe was ritually harvested at this time with a golden sickle and fed to the animals to ensure fertility. It was also valued for its protective properties, particularly against fire and lightning, and was used in medieval times for healing.

Interestingly, once the Christian Church had coopted Yule and other Solstice festivals in its quest for domination, mistletoe was prohibited as a decoration, most likely due to its association with magic.

CELEBRATING YULE

Many covens meet just before dawn on the day of the Solstice to hold their Yule rituals, and then watch the rebirth of the God enacted as the Sun rises. In some traditions, the fires and/or candles are lit in encouragement of the Sun God's emergence, welcoming his returning light. Themes of ritual may include regeneration, light in the darkness, and setting intentions for the new year.

In some Wiccan traditions, this is the time to ritually reenact the battle between the Oak King and the Holly King. These twin brothers represent the opposing poles of the Sun's annual journey through the seasons. The Holly King, representing the dark half of the year, reigns until the Winter Solstice, when he is cut down by the Oak King, who heralds in the beginning of the waxing daylight. This cyclical story serves as a reminder that light and dark are both essential parts of existence in Nature—neither can exist without the other.

For solitary Wiccans who live "double lives" as far as mainstream society is concerned, Yule can be a challenging Sabbat to make time for, swamped as so many are with the obligations of the Christmas season. However, since plenty of the traditions associated with both holidays overlap, it's easy enough to infuse more conventional practices with a little Yule magic.

For example, hang a sprig of holly above your door to ensure protection and good fortune for your family and your guests. Magically charge your Christmas tree ornaments before placing them on the branches. Whisper an incantation to the Goddess over any cookies, spiced cider, or any other holiday goods you make for your friends, family or coworkers. You can spread the blessings of your own personal holiday throughout your community without anyone even knowing it!

For those without indoor hearths, a Yule log can be fashioned from a small tree branch—flatten it on one side so it will sit evenly on the altar and drill small holes to place candles into. Go outside and gather boughs of fir, juniper or cedar, as well as pinecones, holly berries, and any other "natural decor" to bring the energies of protection, prosperity, and renewal into your home.

Use mistletoe to bring peace and healing to your life by placing leaves in a sachet or hanging it over your door. Honor the rebirth of the Sun by inscribing discs, pinwheels, or other solar symbols into a large red, orange or yellow pillar candle. Light it at dawn on the day of the Winter Solstice to welcome the Sun and the new beginning of the Wheel of the Year.

YULE CORRESPONDENCES

Colors: red, green, gold, silver, white, orange

Stones: bloodstone, garnet, emerald, diamond, ruby, clear quartz

Herbs: bayberry, blessed thistle, frankincense, chamomile, mistletoe, ivy, rosemary, all evergreens, oak and holly trees

Flowers: sunflowers, dried flowers from summer

Incense: frankincense, cedar, juniper, pine, cinnamon, myrrh, bayberry

Altar decorations/symbols: candles, evergreen wreaths and boughs, holly, mistletoe, pinecones, Yule log, snowflakes, pinwheels, yellow discs, other solar symbols and imagery

Foods: fruits, nuts, baked goods, cider, spiced cider, eggnog, ginger tea, wassail

INNER LIGHT MEDITATION

No matter which holiday(s) you observe in December, it's hard to avoid the noise and bustle of the general holiday season. The commercialism of mainstream society is at its height, there are many social gatherings to go to, and everything seems to feel busier.

It can be a struggle to stay balanced and grounded at this time, especially for people who are strongly affected by the lack of sunlight at this point in the year. This simple visualization can help you connect with your inner light, your center, where your connection to the divine resides.

Meditation is very helpful for people from all walks of life. For Witches, it's a key tool for cultivating a magical state of mind. Here, the candle is a physical symbol for what you're connecting to on the ethereal plane: your inner flame. Adding a little greenery to the scene, even if it's just a few pine needles, brings in the Earth element as well, but it's not strictly necessary for the meditation.

You will need:

- 1 white votive candle
- Small evergreen (pine, cedar, etc.) branch or bough (optional)

Instructions:

Arrange the evergreen on your altar in a visually pleasing manner.

Light the candle and sit quietly, gazing at the flame for a few moments. Then gently close your eyes.

See the flame as a white light spreading from the center of your heart throughout the rest of your body.

Hold this visualization and breathe deeply and slowly.

When you find you've wandered off in your mind, gently return your focus to the white light suffusing your entire being.

After 5 to 10 minutes, allow the light to relax back into the form of a candle flame sitting in the center of your heart.

When you feel ready, open your eyes. All is well.

MAGICAL YULE BREW

This delicious tea is a nice non-alcoholic alternative to the traditional wassail, though you can turn it into a hot toddy if you like by adding whiskey, brandy or vodka.

Wassail (mulled cider or wine) was originally part of fertility magic among the ancient Norse. It was poured onto the ground at Midwinter to encourage abundant crops in the coming year.

To turn this tea into a magical brew, be sure to charge all ingredients before making it, and say a blessing as you pour the water over the tea and herb mixture. Then drink it in advance of (or during) ritual and/or spellwork.

This recipe is for one cup, but you can adapt it to serve more. Just add one teabag, one lemon slice and one cinnamon stick for each additional person and increase the rest of the ingredients as you see fit.

If you don't have muslin bag or cheesecloth to keep the herbs and spices in while steeping, you can let them float loose in the pot and use a strainer when pouring the tea into mugs. If you don't have a teapot, use a large mug or bowl and cover it with a plate while the tea is steeping.

You will need:

- 1 cup hot (boiled) water
- 1 teabag of black tea
- 1 lemon slice
- 5 whole cloves
- ½ teaspoon dried chamomile
- ¼ teaspoon allspice berries
- Pinch grated ginger

- 1/8 teaspoon orange zest
- 1 cinnamon stick
- Honey to taste
- Muslin bag or square piece of cheesecloth and kitchen twine (optional)
- Teapot
- Mug(s)

Instructions:

Place the herbs and spices except for the lemon, cloves, and cinnamon stick into a muslin bag or cheesecloth sachet.

Place this into the teapot along with the teabag.

Pour the hot water over the tea and herbs and cover, letting steep for 3-5 minutes.

Stud the lemon slice with the cloves.

Pour the steeped tea into the mug and add the lemon slice.

Sweeten with honey and stir with the cinnamon stick. Enjoy!

IMBOLC

Northern Hemisphere: February 1st or 2nd

Southern Hemisphere: August 1st or 2nd

Pronounced: IM-bulk, IM-molg, or imb-OLC

Themes: quickening, hope, renewal, fertility, purification, hearth & home, return of the light

Also known as: Brigid's Day, Oimelc, Feast of Torches, Feast of Pan, Lupercalia, Snowdrop Festival, Feast of the Waxing Light

Although the Spring Equinox is our modern designation for the official beginning of spring, it was Imbolc that traditionally heralded the end of winter in the pagan world.

As the mid-point of the traditional dark half of the year, which begins with Samhain and ends at Beltane, Imbolc marks the time when the grip of winter begins to soften and the Earth starts to come back to life. For people who live in northern climates, where snow and ice dominate the landscape, this is truly a celebration of hope and possibility, as the light grows stronger each day, and subtle signs of the coming of spring begin to emerge.

The days are noticeably lengthening now, as the Sun God's power begins to grow. Among different Wiccan traditions he is described variously as an infant nursing at the Goddess' breast and as a young boy making his way toward maturity. Either way, he is a waxing presence in the sky, higher and more visible with each passing day.

The Goddess, in the form of the Earth, is stirring from her rest following the birth of the God. We see this manifesting as the frozen ground begins to thaw, crocuses and daffodils poke through the surface, and the first birds pass through on their return migration from the southern climates. This is the time when the three-fold aspect of the Goddess shifts from Crone back into Maiden, as the air takes on a hint of youthful energy in the anticipation of warmer days just around the corner.

Our ancestors paid close attention to these early signs of spring. In fact, in the earliest days, the actual date of festival would have been determined by them—for example, once the blackthorns came into bloom.

The cross-quarter day was a time for weather divination in many cultures. In Celtic lore, the length of the winter was determined by the divine hag Cailleach, who would come out to gather the last of her firewood. If she wanted to make the winter last awhile longer, she would make bright, sunny weather on Imbolc—this way she would enjoy a long day of gathering plenty of wood. If she slept through the day, the weather would be gloomy and cold, and the people would know that winter was nearly over.

A Scottish tradition held that Brighid's serpent emerged from under the Earth on Imbolc to test the weather. If it remained above ground, the winter would end soon, but if it returned to its home, another month or more of cold weather was in store. Germanic tribes followed a similar custom with bears and badgers, which in later centuries was adapted to the groundhog and his shadow on Groundhog's Day in the U.S.

Imbolc also marks the beginning of the agricultural season, as the soil is being readied for the first planting and herd animals prepare to give birth. Farmers make needed repairs to their equipment before the season starts in earnest, and rituals for blessing tools and seeds are held at this time—a tradition going back for centuries, if not longer. In every aspect of life—for humans, animals and plants—it's time to start moving around again after the long winter's rest.

The name "Imbolc" itself comes from the ancient Irish and has been translated as "in the belly," referring to the pregnancy of ewes. A related name for the holiday is "Oimelc," meaning "ewe's milk," though this name seems more in use by modern Pagans than it was by the ancient Celts. These milk-producing livestock were crucial for survival for rural people in pre-modern times, especially at this point in the winter, when food stores might be running low or completely empty. So the onset of lambing season was definitely an occasion for celebration!

Purification is another central focus at Imbolc, stemming from the oldest days when dwellings had to be shut tight against the cold for months and bathing was a very infrequent activity. At the first sign of thaw, it was time to throw open the doors, cleanse the house of the stuffy, stale air, and jump into the nearest body of water (once the ice had thawed, of course!). Sunlight was also a purifying force—a manifestation of the Element of Fire—and was taken advantage of as much as possible for renewing the body and the spirit.

BRIGHID, GODDESS OF FIRE

Although each of the cross-quarter days has Celtic roots, Imbolc may be the most Celtic-influenced of the Wiccan Sabbats. While it's true that some forms of Wicca take their inspiration for this holiday from other peoples of pre-Christian Europe, such as the Greeks or the Norse, the most widely used name for is still Imbolc (or "Imbolg," in some areas).

The celebration of Imbolc in Ireland, Scotland and the Isle of Man goes back into pre-written history, and this feast is mentioned in some of the earliest surviving Irish literature. The significance of the cross-quarter day may even predate the Celts themselves, in fact—some of the neolithic monuments in Ireland are actually aligned so that the Sun lights up their inner chambers on this day.

Many Wiccans borrow more than just the name of the Sabbat from the Celts—they also honor the goddess Brighid, who was traditionally the central focus of Imbolc celebrations in Celtic lands. Like the Wiccan goddess, Brighid is three-fold, or "triune" goddess, with aspects that align with the Maiden, Mother and Crone archetypes. In Irish mythology, she rules the three areas of smithcraft, healing and poetry, all of which were powerful activities in Celtic culture.

As a healer, Brighid is associated with many springs and holy wells that were known for their healing, purifying properties. Her cauldron of inspiration sustained poets and bards, and her co-creative powers extended to midwifery and crafting.

Her rule over smithcraft, or metalworking—the alchemical art of transforming raw materials into weaponry and tools—is part of her association with the Element of Fire. In addition, she is said to have been born at sunrise, with a tower of flame bursting from her head and reaching all the way to heaven. She is called "keeper of the sacred flame," and in pre-Christian times her priestesses kept a perpetual fire in her honor at a temple in Kildare, Ireland.

Brighid is also considered the guardian of home and hearth, and was invoked to protect the herds and assist in providing a fruitful harvest. She was associated with the cow, a symbol of motherhood and life sustenance, as well as with the light half of the year, so her presence at this time in late winter was very important to the people.

On Imbolc Eve, Brighid was said to visit the households of those who invited her, and bestow blessings on the inhabitants. Various customs for inviting her were practiced throughout the lands where she was worshipped.

The most common included making her a bed out of a basket with white bedding, and making a straw doll-like figure of Brighid (called a Brídeóg). These corn dollies, as they are also called, were carried from door to door so each household could offer a gift to the goddess.

Families would have a special meal and save some of the food and drink to leave outside for Brighid, along with clothing or strips of cloth for her to bless. The following morning, the family would inspect the ashes of their smoored fire for any marks that showed Brighid had indeed entered the house. The cloth would be brought back inside, now imbued with healing and protective powers.

"Brighid's crosses" were also made from stalks of wheat, formed into a square, an equilateral cross, or an ancient protection symbol resembling a counter-clockwise swastika that was found in various cultures throughout the ancient world. These were hung over the entrances of homes and stables to

45

protect the household from fire, lightning, and any threat to the animals and the harvest. The crosses would be left hanging throughout the year, until the following Imbolc, and are still used in some places today.

Brighid was such a central part of Irish pagan culture that the Christian Church eventually turned her into a saint as part of their religious conquest, and Imbolc is known throughout Ireland as "Brighid's Day." The cross-quarter day was further coopted across Europe by the invention of Candlemas, a Christian holy day that involved the making and blessing of candles for the coming year. Many Wiccans and other Pagans with less specifically-Celtic leanings also use the name Candlemas for this Sabbat.

CELEBRATING IMBOLC

Fire plays a big role in most Wiccan Imbolc traditions. At coven celebrations, a high priestess may wear a crown of lit candles or carry tapers during ritual. This is done in honor of the Goddess stepping into her Maiden aspect and the God's growth into boyhood.

Candles are lit in each room of the house to welcome the Sun. Bonfires are held if the weather is fair, and any evergreen decorations from the Yule Sabbat are burned as a way of letting go of the past season, or even the past year.

For Wiccans, Brighid's status as a Fire goddess makes her an appropriate deity to be recognized on this Sabbat that celebrates the return of the Sun. You can honor her in a variety of ways—by visiting a natural spring or holy well and making offerings, cleaning and purifying your home, lighting candles for her at your altar, or even engaging in writing or other creative activities.

Try making a Brídeóg to place on your altar, and make a Brighid's bed for her to rest in. If you made a "Corn Mother" for Lammas last year, you can repurpose it, dressing her this time in white, yellow or pink (think "Maiden" colors). The bed can be a small basket, a wooden box, or even a well-decorated shoe box. Just be sure to make it comfortable and attractive, with blankets and flowers, ribbons, etc.

Place your Brídeóg in the bed near your hearth (or altar, if you don't have a fireplace). Some traditions leave a small wand with her, which she can use to bless your home. You can also make your own Brighid's cross to hang over your doorway. Instructions for these Imbolc crafts can be easily found online or in other print sources.

Other traditional Imbolc activities include going for walks or hikes to look for signs of spring in the surrounding countryside, taking a ritual bath for physical and energetic purification, and decorating and blessing farm equipment (such as ploughs) for the coming season. Placing a besom, or ritual broom, by the front door symbolizes sweeping out the stale energy of winter and allowing fresh new energy to enter your home and your life.

As with all cross-quarter Sabbats, a special feast is a great idea, particularly on Feb 1st, or "Imbolc Eve." Bringing food to those in need after the long winter—such as homeless shelters and elderly shut-ins—is an excellent way to raise abundance energy for your community.

Finally, Imbolc is a good time to perform self-dedication rituals, or to undergo coven initiation if you are in a position to do so.

IMBOLC CORRESPONDENCES

<u>Colors:</u> red, white, yellow, pink

<u>Stones:</u> garnet, ruby, onyx, bloodstone, amethyst

<u>Herbs:</u> angelica, basil, bay leaf, myrrh, coltsfoot, heather

<u>Flowers:</u> snowdrops, violets, crocus, daffodils, forsythia

<u>Incense:</u> myrrh, cinnamon, violet, wisteria, jasmine, vanilla

<u>Altar decorations/symbols:</u> white flowers, potted bulbs, Brighid's cross, Brídeóg, sheep, cows, ploughs, cauldron, poems or poetry book, candles or candle wheel

<u>Foods:</u> pumpkin and sunflower seeds, poppyseed pastries, dairy products, early spring vegetables

HEARTH AND HOME PURIFICATION RITUAL

You don't have to be a Witch to notice that the energy and mood of a home is always improved by a thorough cleaning. But making a magical experience out of it takes it to a whole new level!

If you need to do this cleaning in stages, start a couple of days ahead of time. Then put the finishing touches on your cleaning job right before the ritual.

You will need:

- Bowl of water
- Rosemary essential oil or fresh / dried rosemary
- 1 blue candle
- Smudge stick of sage and lavender or sweetgrass

Instructions:

First, clean your house from top to bottom.

This includes the kitchen, which is the modern-day "hearth" for people who don't have working fireplaces in their homes. Clear away any cobwebs lurking in neglected corners, dust and wipe down all surfaces, sweep, mop, vacuum, etc. For best results, use all-natural cleaning agents made with essential oils, rather than chemical products.

Be sure to give extra attention to any ritual/magical objects such as your altar, tools, crystals, etc. If you've been hanging onto any charms or other magical crafts that seem to have finished serving their purpose, now is a good time to respectfully dispose of them.

If weather permits, keep a window open or a door cracked while you clean, and be sure to listen to music that puts you in a happy mood.

When the house is ready, light the candle. Add 3 drops of rosemary to the water and say the following (or similar) words:

"I give thanks to the purifying essence of Fire.
I give thanks to the purifying essence of Water.
I call on them to bless and protect this home.
So let it be."

Place the blessed water in front of the candle.

Light the smudge bundle and carry it through each room in the house.

Walk in a clockwise motion, wafting the smoke into every corner.

Open the doors and windows as much as possible, and be sure to keep the front door open for at least a few minutes after the smudging. (This allows any unwanted energy to exit your home.)

Finally, sprinkle a few drops of the rosemary water over the windowsills and doorways in each room.

The candle can be left to burn out on its own, or snuffed and lit again later for ordinary uses.

IMBOLC SEED
AND CANDLE SPELL

This spell draws on the symbolic power of seeds at the center of the "hearth" created by three candles. The candles represent the three-fold realms of Brighid, but calling on her directly for assistance isn't required. (But if you feel a connection with her, then by all means ask!) Use this spell to set the tone for the coming growing season in the realms of creativity, healing and abundance.

To prepare, spend some time identifying your goals. You might have three separate goals, such as finding new ideas and energy for a creative project; addressing a physical or emotional injury; and securing a new home. Or, you may have one goal that can be related to each of these domains in some way. You may want to do some journaling and/or meditating to help you clarify what you want to manifest at this time.

If possible, take a ritual bath before working this spell. As always, feel free to tailor the words to suit your own style and beliefs.

You will need:

- 1 yellow Goddess candle
- 1 red God candle
- 3 white spell candles or tea lights
- Small handful (or seed packet) of basil, pumpkin or sunflower seeds
- Small ceramic, stone, glass or wooden bowl

Instructions:

Set up your altar with Imbolc-themed items and imagery.

When you're ready to start, light the Goddess candle and say "*I welcome and give thanks to the awakening Earth.*"

Light the God candle and say "*I welcome and give thanks to the strengthening Sun.*"

Place the seeds into the bowl (if they're in a packet, pour them out).

Hold the bowl in your hands for a moment. Visualize sending your personal power into each seed. See the bowl filling with light in your mind's eye.

Raise the bowl toward the sky and charge the seeds with your voice by saying "*Through these seeds of the Earth will come many blessings.*"

Now place the bowl on the altar and arrange the three white candles around it in a triangle shape. The candle at the top of the triangle represents inspiration. The bottom right candle is for healing, and the bottom left for abundance.

Light the top candle and say: "*By the power of the word I am inspired to right action.*"

Light the right-hand candle and say: "*By the healing waters of the well I am purified.*"

Light the left-hand candle and say: "*By the fire of the forge I create my abundance.*"

Now spend a few moments gazing upon your work. Give thanks again to the Goddess and the God. If you like, seal your spell with the words "*It is done*" or "*Blessed Be.*"

Leave the bowl in place until the candles have burned all the way down.

Save the seeds for planting when it's appropriate to do so. You can also include them in any kind of abundance charm/sachet or else scatter them over the Earth outside of your home.

OSTARA
(SPRING EQUINOX)

<u>Northern Hemisphere:</u> March 19-21

<u>Southern Hemisphere:</u> September 20-23

<u>Pronounced:</u> OH-star-ah

<u>Themes:</u> balance, renewal, action, beginnings, hope, new possibilities

<u>Also known as:</u> Alban Eiler, Rites of Spring, Eostra's Day, Vernal Equinox, March Equinox, Spring Equinox, Lady Day, Bacchanalia

As the first solar Sabbat of the calendar year, Ostara marks the Spring Equinox, one of two points in the Sun's journey at which day and night are of equal length.

The Sun has crossed the "celestial equator," and will shine on Earth for longer each day until it reaches its zenith at the Summer Solstice. For Earth's inhabitants, this is a fortuitous moment, as the scarcity of winter comes to an end and the growing season begins in earnest. On the modern calendar, this is the first day of spring.

Depending on where you live, there may still be snow on the ground, but the Earth is beginning to thaw and rivers rise and overflow their banks. Green grass and spring flowers emerge, lambs, rabbits and chicks are born, and the promise of further new life is felt on the breeze, which is milder than it was just a few weeks ago.

The waxing light is truly felt now, as the Sun's power seems to quicken. The lengthening of the days, first perceived at Imbolc, seem to be growing at an even faster rate as the Sun sets later and further north with each passing day. But just at this moment, the light and the dark exist in equal measure, and this gives Ostara its primary theme of balance.

This balance is observed not only between night and day, but also generally in weather patterns—the harsh, bitter cold of winter is behind us and the relentless heat of summer has yet to arrive. In colder climates, it's not unusual for spring and winter to take turns during these days, with one day feeling more like February and the next more like May. Nonetheless, the fertility of the Earth becomes more and more undeniable as the slow energies of winter give way to the fresh new vibrancy of spring.

This is a time to reunite with the Earth in a tactile way after many months spent largely indoors. Gardening begins in earnest now, as soil is prepared and seed trays are set out in the sunlight to sprout. Those who practice green Witchcraft may perform seed-blessing rituals if they did not already do so at Imbolc.

Magical gardens are plotted out in order to grow the herbs, flowers and vegetables that will later be harvested for feasting, ritual and spellwork. As the first green shoots poke up through the soil, we truly begin the active half of the Wheel of the Year, turning our focus to outward action until the inward, passive half begins again at the Autumn Equinox.

Ostara is also a time to reflect on the balance between the male and female energies of the Universe, each of which requires the other to exist. This gender polarity is at the heart of traditional Wicca, with the Goddess and the God in constant co-creation throughout the changing of the seasons. At this point on the Wheel, the Goddess of the Earth is in her fertile Maiden aspect, while the Sun God grows into his maturity. There is a youthful joy between the two as they make their forays into romance and desire.

In some Wiccan traditions, this is considered the time when the divine pair comes together to conceive the next incarnation of the God, who will be born nine months later at Yule. In many others, the coupling of the divine pair happens at Beltane, when the new energies of growth and light have progressed further into wild abundance. Nonetheless, in Nature we see the mating of animals and insects is well underway as "spring fever" takes hold.

FERTILITY AND THE GODDESS OF THE DAWN

As midpoints of the solar year, the equinoxes were not typically as widely celebrated as the solstices in pagan Europe. However, there are megalithic sites in Great Britain that align with the Sun on this day, as there are in many other parts of the world.

Many ancient cultures in the Mediterranean region did hold festivals during this time, such as Sham el-Nessim, an Egyptian holiday which celebrates the beginning of spring and can be traced back almost 5,000 years. In Persia, the festival of Nowruz, (meaning "new day") marked the Spring Equinox, and the Jewish calendar sets the dates for Passover based on where the New Moon falls in relation to this day.

In northern Europe, the Latvian festival of Lieldienas was a pre-Christian equinox holiday before it was absorbed into the Christian Easter. And the Norse pagans are said to have honored their female deities with a festival called Dísablót, though some sources place this holiday at the Autumn Equinox or closer to Imbolc.

The Scandinavian tribes and the Anglo-Saxons are where most of our modern Ostara traditions come from, most particularly in the name of this Sabbat. A Saxon goddess named Eostre (also spelled Eostra) is described by an 8th-century scholar who mentions a feast held in her honor at springtime. Little is known about her, and even less is known about her Germanic equivalent, Ostara, for whom the month of April was named in ancient Germanic languages.

However, many place names in some Scandinavian countries suggest that this goddess was fairly widely worshipped before the Christianization of Europe. The name "Eostre" has been translated as "east," "dawn," and "morning light," and so she has seemed a fitting deity to honor at the beginning of the growing season, even if much of the symbolism and lore about her in modern Wicca and other forms of Paganism has essentially been borrowed from other, better-known goddesses like the Norse Freya.

Symbols and customs of Ostara are recognizable to many as being part of the "Easter" season, such as the rabbit or hare and the egg—both symbols of fertility. The hare—a larger, more rural relative of the rabbit—is believed to be an ancient symbol of the Earth goddess archetype. Hares were also associated with the Moon, and in some places with witches, who were thought to be able to transform themselves into these quick-moving animals.

The fertility association is fairly obvious, as rabbits are known for their fast and prolific reproductive abilities. But there is also an element of honoring the Sun through hare symbolism, as these animals are usually nocturnal, but come out into the daylight during Spring to find their mates. Rabbits and eggs have traditionally gone together, both in ancient days and in modern Easter customs. This stems from our pagan ancestors' observations that plover eggs could sometimes be found in abandoned hares' "nests" in the wild.

The egg itself was a potent symbol of new beginnings and the promise of coming manifestations in many cultures. Painted eggs were part of the ancient Persian Nowruz celebrations, and egg hunts have been traced back at least 2,000 years to Indian and Asian spring customs.

In Anglo-Saxon England, eggs were buried in gardens and under barns as a form of fertility and abundance magic. Offerings of eggs were made to female deities in ancient Scandinavia and in Germany. Interestingly, the egg also speaks to the theme of balance at Ostara, through the tradition of standing an egg on its end in the moments right around the exact time of the Equinox.

Of all the Sabbats, Ostara is the most clear example of how the Christian Church went about converting the pagan populations of northern Europe. By choosing the spring for its own celebration of renewal (in the form of the resurrection of Jesus) and adopting the name of this older festival, it effectively absorbed and dissolved this and other Spring Equinox holidays.

However, as with Yule and Samhain, the old pagan customs and traditions have stubbornly stuck around, and are even widely practiced in mainstream society.

CELEBRATING OSTARA

As the weather grows warmer, Ostara is a particularly wonderful time to get outdoors and take in the seasonal changes taking place all around you. If you haven't been in the habit of truly noticing spring's unfolding before, choose a place to visit regularly and study the transformation of the trees and other plant life.

Greet the bees and other insects with joy as they begin to appear, and thank them for their role in sustaining life. Take every opportunity you can to watch the Sun set just a little later each evening. And if you don't already have a garden to prepare, consider starting one—even if you only have a windowsill to grow a magical herb or two.

Coven rituals often focus on the goddess Ostara or another goddess of spring. Witches may meet just before dawn to watch the Sun rise on this perfectly balanced day. Dyeing eggs is a fun activity to do with fellow Wiccans, perhaps using color correspondences to create magical eggs for later spellwork.

Natural objects are always a welcome part of rituals at any time of the year, but especially at the Spring Equinox, the first Sabbat after winter when flowers, buds and blossoms are truly available to be gathered. Sprinkle petals around your altar, float them on water in your cauldron, and wear them in your hair if you like, but be careful to harvest spring wildflowers responsibly, as they serve as much-needed food sources for our much-needed pollinators!

OSTARA CORRESPONDENCES

Colors: yellow, light green, light pink, blue, all pastel shades

Stones: amethyst, aquamarine, jasper, moonstone, rose quartz

Herbs: Irish moss, lemongrass, meadowsweet, catnip, spearmint, cleavers, dogwood and ash trees, woodruff

Flowers: daffodils, honeysuckle, iris, violets, Easter lilies, roses, dandelions, tulips, lilacs

Incense: jasmine, rose, violet, lotus, magnolia, ginger, sage, strawberry, lemon

Altar decorations/symbols: spring flowers, seeds, potted plants, colored eggs, rabbits/hares, birds, pinwheels, yellow discs, other solar symbols and imagery, ladybugs, bumblebees

Foods: eggs, honey, sprouts, dandelion greens, strawberries, all spring vegetables, pumpkin and sunflower seeds, pine nuts

BARK AND FLOWER BALANCING SPELL

Both the Spring and the Fall Equinoxes provide excellent opportunities to work for balance in our lives. This can mean achieving better physical health, learning how to deal more skillfully with an emotional challenge, or balancing the monthly budget.

Anything you're dealing with that's hindering your ability to make progress in the outer world is a good area to focus on releasing, so that the energies of positive manifestation have more room to come into your life. For best results, identify a goal that aligns with the physical, mental or emotional realm in order to take full advantage of the magical correspondences of your chosen spring flower.

As for the bark, this should be gleaned (i.e. gathered from the ground) and *not* cut from a living tree. Many trees actively shed their bark at the onset of spring in order to make room for their own new growth.

Trees associated with establishing balance include ash, birch, cedarwood, poplar, willow and white oak. If none of these grow where you live, look up the magical correspondences of the trees that do grow in your area, or ask the God and Goddess to guide you in finding the right bark for this spell.

Flowers used in balancing magic include:

Mental: daffodil, iris, lilac, violet (yellow candle)
Emotional: crocus, daffodil, iris, violet, tulip (pink or light blue candle)
Physical: alpine aster, iris, honeysuckle, lilac (green/light green candle)

You will need:

- Piece of gleaned bark
- Handful of flower petals
- Spell candle in a color corresponding to your goal
- Pencil (or ink and quill)

Instructions:

Start by meditating on your goal.

What does *balance* in this situation or area of your life look and feel like to you? Identify a word or short phrase that encapsulates the achievement of your goal, such as "optimal health," "harmony in the home" or "all bills paid."

Write this on the bark. Don't worry if the pencil lead doesn't show up, as the letters are still being traced into the essence of the bark's energy.

Light the candle and lay the bark on your altar or work space.

Sprinkle the daffodils around the bark in a circle three times, moving clockwise.

With each rotation, say the following (or similar) words:

> *"As the day is balanced with the night,*
> *and the darkness balanced with the light,*
> *I find balance in my life."*

Allow the candle to burn out on its own.

Within 24 hours, return the bark to the Earth, either where you found it or another place in Nature.

OSTARA EGG
GARDEN FERTILITY SPELL

Many cultures around the world have long traditions of using eggs in magic, for healing, divination, protection and other purposes. Here, the properties of fertility and promise inherent to the egg is combined with the same energies that are so magnified at the height of Spring.

For those already preparing their gardens, this is a highly opportune time to work this spell, as you're already out digging in the soil! But if you don't have a garden, shift the focus to creating an abundant and thriving home, and bury the egg in your yard.

You will need:

- 1 hard-boiled egg
- Green marker or green paint and brush

Instructions:

Boil the egg with the specific intention for this spell. You might even say a blessing over the water before you start.

When the egg is dry and cool enough, draw a symbol of abundance appropriate to your goal—a flower or other plant, a house, a dollar sign or even the Sun.

Once the symbol is dry, hold the egg in your hands and raise it toward the sky. Say the following (or similar) words:

*"As the light and warmth increase,
so does the bounty of my life.
So let it be."*

Bury the egg in your garden or somewhere near the front door, visualizing golden light radiating from the egg throughout the soil, nourishing the roots of your growing plants or the foundation of your home.

BELTANE

Northern Hemisphere: April 30 or May 1

Southern Hemisphere: Oct 31 or Nov 1

Pronounced: bee-YAWL-tinnuh, or BELL-tinnuh

Themes: passion, mischief, sensuality, sexuality, beauty, romance, fertility, vitality, abundance

Also known as: May Day, Walpurgisnacht, Floralia, Calan Mai

By the time May 1st arrives in the Northern Hemisphere, spring is truly in full swing and the balance is tipping toward summer. The heat of the Sun increases with each day, and the Earth turns ever-deepening shades of green as buds and blossoms give way to the emerging new leaves. Flowers seem to explode along the roadsides while birds, bees, and other flying creatures fill the air. And even if a stray chill sneaks back in for a day or two around this time, there's still no going back—winter is decidedly over.

In fact, May 1st marked the official beginning of the light half of the year in pre-modern times, making this day the official beginning of summer for our Celtic ancestors. Indeed, Beltane—or May Day as it is also known—is a time for exuberant celebration, as the long, warm days and the lush abundance of the growing season are ramping up. The hopeful feeling that was kindled at Imbolc and built upon at Ostara now comes into full fruition.

Wiccans recognize Beltane as a time to celebrate the return of passion, vitality, fun and frivolity, and the co-creative energies of Nature that are so evident at this time of year. By this point all living creatures have come out of hibernation and are enjoying the sunshine and the mild days.

"Spring fever" is at its peak, as people find themselves unable to concentrate on their work or studies and long instead to spend all their time outdoors. Primal urges toward lust and wildness become stronger and we see both animals and humans pairing off, sparked by that most basic of instincts: to reproduce.

This life-giving relationship between masculine and feminine energies is honored now, perhaps more directly at this Sabbat than at any other point on the Wheel of the Year. In the cyclical story of the Goddess and the God, this is the shift between their mother-child relationship to that of partners in co-creation.

Over the spring months, the God has matured into his young manhood, and the Goddess is again ready to step from her Maiden aspect into the life-giving Mother. In their prime of life they fall in love and unite, and the Goddess once again becomes pregnant, ensuring the rebirth of the God after the current growing season comes to an end in the autumn.

This is the act that brings about new life in the form of abundant crops, healthy livestock, and forests full of wild game and healing herbs. It is the fundamental building block of the continuation of life, and so is celebrated joyfully at this time by Wiccans and other Pagans alike. In some traditions, the union between the Goddess and God is seen as a divine marriage, and so handfastings—or Wiccan weddings—are customary at this time.

In addition to the Sun God and/or the Horned God, many Wiccans and other Pagans recognize an aspect of the God in the Green Man, an archetypal image of a male face camouflaged by leafy foliage. This mysterious face is found carved into very old buildings throughout Europe, including cathedrals, and is often connected with the Celtic god Cernunnos; however, variations of the image have been discovered all over the world. In early May, as leaves begin to emerge from the trees and shrubs, the return of the Green Man is imminent.

Soon the summer foliage will hide all that was visible during the bare months of winter, and we are reminded of the divinity hidden within plain sight that this greenery so often evokes. Perhaps for this reason, Beltane is also a time of the faeries, who are considered to be more active on this day than any other except for Samhain, which sits directly opposite the Wheel from Beltane.

Faery traditions can be traced back to the Irish *Aos Sí*, a name often translated as "faeries" or "spirits," but are found in various forms throughout ancient pagan cultures. They are said to inhabit various places in Nature, from hills and forests to small plants and flowers. Wiccans who are sensitive to the presence of faeries will leave offerings for them on Beltane Eve.

THE LIGHTING OF THE BALEFIRE

The name "Beltane" has been traced back to an old Celtic word meaning "bright fire," and is thought by some scholars to be related to the ancient Sun god Belenos, whose name has been translated as "bright shining one." Belenos was worshipped throughout Celtic Europe and his feast day was on May 1st, so this connection seems logical, but is not universally accepted by historians.

For one thing, Belenos (also known as Bel or Beil) doesn't make significant appearances in the mythology of the areas where Beltane was historically celebrated: Ireland, Scotland, and the Isle of Mann. In fact, he was much more significant to the Gaulish Celts of the European continent, where the May 1st festivals are known by different names. Nonetheless, the ritual importance of fire was a central focus of Beltane for the ancient Celts of the western-most islands, where the first references to the holiday are found.

The chief event at Beltane in ancient Ireland was the lighting of the balefire on the eve of May 1, the first fire of the light half of the Celtic year. In preparation for this event, every household hearth was extinguished.

Legend has it that tribal representatives from all over Ireland met at the hill of Uisneach, a sacred site where a giant bonfire was lit. Each representative would light a torch from the great fire, and carry it back to their village, where the people waited in the darkness. From the village torch, each household would then relight their home fires, so that all of Ireland was set alight from the same initial flame.

In another version of this story, the fire at Uisneach could be seen from several miles away in every direction, signaling to the surrounding villages to light their own central fires, which was then spread throughout their communities. Either way, this act marked the beginning of summer, with hopes for plentiful sunshine throughout the season.

As a living symbol of the Sun, ritual fire was clearly seen as having magical powers. In many Celtic areas, the Beltane fires were also used for ritual purification of cattle before they were turned out into the summer pastures. The cattle were driven between two large bonfires, which were tended by Druids who used special incantations to imbue the fires with sacred energy.

The fire would clear the animals of any lingering winter disease and protect them from illness and accidents throughout the summer. People would also walk between the fires, or jump over them, for luck and fertility through the coming year. In some areas, the ashes from the smoldering fire would be sprinkled over crops, livestock, and the people themselves.

Over time, the annual Beltane fires grew into larger festivals, where people came to greet each other after the long winter. Dancing, music, games and great feasts became traditions, along with a free license for sexual promiscuity on this special occasion. Other customs observed at this time included eating "Beltane bannock"—a special oatcake that bestowed an abundant growing season and protection of livestock—and making a "May Bush," a branch or bough from a tree decorated with brightly colored ribbons, flowers, and egg shells.

People would dance around the May Bush on Beltane, and then either place it by the front door for luck or burn it in the bonfire. This was believed to be a remnant of Druidic tradition, which held many trees to be sacred and possess magical qualities. A related custom was hanging a rowan branch over the hearth or weaving it into the ceiling to protect the house for the coming year.

Trees, herbs and flowers in general played a part at Beltane and at other May Day celebrations throughout Europe.

Primrose flowers and hawthorne and hazel blossoms were gathered and placed at doors and windows, made into garlands, and even used to adorn cattle. Yellow flowers were prized for their association with the Sun.

Herbs gathered on this day were said to be especially potent for magic and healing, especially if gathered at dawn or while the morning dew was still on them. The "May dew" inspired a variety of traditions around beauty. Young women would roll naked in the dew or collect it to wash their faces with, as it was said to purify the skin, maintain youthful looks and help attract a love partner.

CELEBRATING BELTANE

Today's Beltane celebrations draw from various traditions across the pagan landscape of Europe. And while bonfires are definitely a big part of most rituals, Wiccan and other Pagan observances don't necessarily borrow as heavily from Celtic lore at Beltane as they do at Imbolc or Samhain.

More typically, the public celebrations incorporate traditions from Germanic cultures—especially dancing around the Maypole. This is the very tall, circular pole made ideally from wood that features in many May Day festivities, both Pagan and secular alike. At the top of the pole hang ribbons of various colors, and the participants each hold one ribbon as they circle the pole in an interweaving dance, until the length of it is decorated.

This practice is rooted in customs found in England, where the cross-quarter day is known as May Day. The Maypole would be erected in the center of the village, or in a nearby field, and decorated with flowers and branches brought in from the fields, gardens and forests. The villagers would rise at dawn to gather these symbols of summer, and used them to decorate their homes and their bodies as well. Women would braid flowers into their hair, and both men and women—especially those who were young and unmarried—put extra effort into grooming themselves for the big day.

It was traditionally young people who did the dancing around the Maypole, and any woman who wanted to conceive a child was sure to be among them. In the earliest times, the dancing would have been a looser, simpler affair. The more intricately involved dance with the entwining ribbons came about relatively recently, in the 19th century.

Wiccans and other Pagans recognize the pole itself as a supremely phallic symbol, representing the God at the height of his powers. The garlands and greenery symbolize the Goddess and her fertility. As the dancers come together, the ribbons gradually encircle the pole until it is symbolically wrapped in the womb of the Earth. In this way, the union between the divine pair is enacted by the whole community.

This association with phallic symbolism is a somewhat recent development, however. Historians believe that the Maypole originated with fertility rituals of ancient Germanic tribes, who would at one time have been dancing around a young living tree as opposed to a cut pole. The tradition evolved over the centuries after being brought to England, where in the 17th century a mistaken association was made between the Maypole and the bawdier customs of ancient Rome. The phallic symbolism has been part of the lore of May Day ever since, especially among Witches.

Covens have bonfires when possible, often lighting a candle first to represent the 'old fire' of the past seasons. The candle is extinguished, and the bonfire ushers in the 'new fire'—the new energies of the coming year. These energies are typically masculine, but there is also a focus on the cauldron as a symbol of the Goddess.

The gender polarity of Wicca is especially evident at Beltane, and the sexual union of the God and Goddess is symbolically enacted through the joining of the athame with the chalice. Literal coupling—or the Great Rite—is also practiced, though not as commonly. It should be pointed out that as Wicca becomes more expansive, some traditions are less focused on gender polarity in order to accommodate the perspectives of gay and transgender people.

The rich lore surrounding Beltane makes for an abundance of ways to celebrate this Sabbat. A fire is appropriate, whether it's an outdoor bonfire, a small fire in a cauldron or heat resistant bowl, or a host of lit candles. Decorate your altar and your home with green branches and flowers gathered in the early morning, and fill a cauldron or large bowl with water and float fresh blossom petals on top.

It's a good time for beauty rituals, so concoct a facial scrub or mask with dried herbs and fresh water from a stream or spring, or braid your hair to represent the coming together of the Goddess and the God. Make an offering of nuts, berries and fruit for the faeries and leave it under a tree in your yard or in the woods. Tie colored ribbons to young tree branches to make wishes for the coming season. Spend some time with your lover outdoors or work magic to bring a lover into your life. Above all, enjoy the warmth in the air and the accelerating growth of the natural world!

BELTANE CORRESPONDENCES

Colors: light and deep greens, yellow, light blue, red and white for the God and Goddess

Stones: malachite, amber, orange carnelian, sapphire, rose quartz

Herbs: birch trees, hawthorn, honeysuckle, rosemary

Flowers: yellow cowslip, lily of the valley, lilac, hyacinth, daisies, roses

Incense: lilac, frankincense, jasmine, African violet, sage, mugwort

Altar decorations/symbols: Maypole, ribbons, garlands, spring flowers, young plants, Goddess and God statues

Foods: oatmeal cakes, bannock and other bread, dairy foods, strawberries, cherries, spring greens

BELTANE
ABUNDANCE DIVINATION

The core theme of Beltane is the fruitful abundance created by the union of the Goddess and the God. You can ask these divine energies for wisdom in helping you manifest your own personal abundance during the coming season.

This is also a great opportunity to deepen your personal relationship with the deities, by simply talking with them in your own words for awhile before pouring the wax. You can use different colors for the deity candles, such as orange and green, if that resonates more with you.

You will need:

- 1 red candle (God)
- 1 white candle (Goddess)
- 1 work candle (optional)
- Small heat-proof plate

Instructions:

Light the work candle, if using.

Place the plate between the two deity candles.

Light the Goddess candle, speaking words of greeting to her as you do so. (You can look up some invocations or simply freestyle it in your own way.)

Light the God candle and greet him in a similar manner.

Spend some time talking to your deities about your hopes for the coming season. Ask any questions you have about any abundance-related issues or developments in your life.

When the candles have accumulated enough melted wax, pick them up together and gently tilt them over the plate, pouring in overlapping circles so that the colors mingle together.

You may want to do this a few times as the candles continue to burn lower.

When the wax has dried, look carefully for images and symbols that can point you in the direction of your stated goals.

HERBAL CHARM
FOR FINDING ROMANCE

Beltane is a great time to work magic for new love. This charm is for single people who don't currently have a love prospect in mind. Be careful not to misuse it as a "snare" for someone you have your eye on, or it will backfire!

If you're handy with a needle and thread, you can add power to the charm by sewing your own sachet in the shape of a heart, but the drawstring bag will work just fine.

You will need:

- 1 teaspoon lavender
- 1 teaspoon hibiscus
- 1 teaspoon damiana
- ¼ inch piece cinnamon stick
- Small drawstring bag (ideally red or pink)
- Small piece of rose quartz and/or garnet

Instructions:

Pour the herbs into a small cauldron or bowl.

Mix together with your fingertips to work your personal energy into the herbs.

Stir three times, clockwise, with the cinnamon stick.

Then pour the herb mixture into the bag and add the stones.

As you close up the charm, say the following (or similar) words:

"Herb and stone,
Flesh and bone,
Bring new love
into my home"

Keep the charm in your bedroom, and bring it with you when you go out in public until you meet your next romantic partner.

LITHA
(SUMMER SOLSTICE)

<u>Northern Hemisphere:</u> June 20-22

<u>Southern Hemisphere:</u> December 20-23

<u>Pronounced:</u> LEE-tha

<u>Themes:</u> abundance, growth, masculine energy, love, magic

<u>Also known as</u>: Midsummer, Midsummer's Eve, Gathering Day, St. John's Day, St. John's Eve, Summer Solstice, Alban Hefin, Feill-Sheathain

Litha, also known in the wider Pagan world as Midsummer, is celebrated on the day of the Summer Solstice—the longest day and shortest night of the solar year.

This is the height of summer, when the days are warm and plentiful. Abundance can be found everywhere—the crops are in full growth as we get closer to the beginning of the harvest season, and the fields and forests are bursting with animal and plant life.

The Sun reaches its highest point, which means the days will now begin to grow shorter again until we reach the Winter Solstice at Yule. But there's no need to think about winter just now—instead, we celebrate our place on this warm and lively side of the Wheel.

This is the time of the God's greatest power, whether we focus on the light and heat of his Sun God aspect; his role as the Green Man, lush with thick foliage; or the Horned God, strong and agile at the heart of the forest. There is a potent masculine energy to be tapped here, if we wish.

At the same time, the Goddess is in her Mother aspect, as the generous Earth yields abundant blessings of food, flowers, and striking natural beauty. We feel the love of this divine pair easily and often in these easy, breezy days of Midsummer.

Magical and medicinal herbs are said to be at the height of their power, and are traditionally gathered on this day to be dried and stored for use in the winter. Many people also feel the energies of the faeries at this time—a slightly mischievous "something" in the air that Shakespeare once captured in *A Midsummer Night's Dream*.

THE POWER OF THE SUN

Many Pagan sources regarding Litha assert that the Celts celebrated Midsummer in much the same way that they observed their four cross-quarter festivals, but there isn't much evidence to support this idea. Nonetheless, the number of Neolithic stone monuments found throughout Europe that align with the Sun on this day—in both Celtic and non-Celtic lands—indicates that the Summer Solstice was indeed significant to our ancient ancestors.

The most well-known example is Stonehenge in England, where from the center of the circle, the Midsummer Sun can be seen rising over the giant Heel Stone. Today, Pagans of many different traditions gather at Stonehenge on the eve of the Summer Solstice, celebrating throughout the night as they await the sunrise. However, it's unlikely that any of the rituals taking place in modern times are connected to the actual history of Stonehenge.

When it comes to the activities of the ancient Germanic tribes, however, much more is known. Particularly in the northernmost regions of Europe, the solstice would have been great cause for celebration, as the near-endless daylight of the height of summer made for such contrast with the long, dark winters.

In a world without electricity and artificial lighting, the Sun's light would have been unimaginably precious. We can see this in the fire-centered traditions that have come down from Norse, Anglo-Saxon, and other Germanic peoples and are still practiced today. Many of these have inspired the Litha celebrations of Wiccans and other modern Pagans.

Aside from the Sun, and to a lesser extent the Moon, fire was the only source of light available to people until the 19th century. Fire is the symbolic manifestation of the Sun on Earth. It is both tangible and untouchable, miraculous yet dangerous, and it demands respect.

Our pagan ancestors—the Norse in particular—honored the Element of Fire at Midsummer with bonfires and torchlight processions, parading with their families, communities and even animals to their ritual sites for the evening's celebrations. The fires were believed to keep away evil spirits and misfortune. In Anglo-Saxon tradition, boys would roam the fields with their torches to drive away dragons who threatened their springs and wells.

A long-standing tradition in many parts of Europe was the "sunwheel," a giant wagon wheel, tar barrel or ball of straw that was set alight and rolled down a steep hill into a river or other body of water. The significance of this ritual has several possible interpretations. Some suggest it symbolized the annual journey of the Sun—after reaching the zenith of the solstice, it now makes its way back down toward its lowest point at Yule. Others believe it encouraged a natural balance between the Elements of Fire and Water, acknowledging the need for rain to nourish the crops and prevent drought.

The Solstice is still observed today throughout Northern Europe with a variety of rituals dating back to pre-Christian times. Bonfires are held on beaches or near waterways in Denmark and Finland, while in Poland, young girls throw wreaths of flowers into the lakes, rivers, and the Baltic Sea.

In many of these countries, the celebrations begin in the evening and last throughout the night until the Sun rises the following morning. In many places, the day is known as St. John's Day, having been appropriated (like most pagan feasts) by the Christian Church. Nonetheless, the pagan roots of the holiday are still clearly recognizable.

The name "Litha" is a modern innovation, borrowed by Wiccans from an old Saxon word for this time of year. The more traditional "Midsummer" is also used by many Wiccans and other Pagans, as this date truly falls in the middle of the summer, despite the fact that our modern calendars designate this as the start of the season.

CELEBRATING LITHA

If there's one thing you should definitely put on your Litha "to do" list, it's to get outdoors and enjoy the summer weather! Even if your actual ritual must be held inside, you can prepare yourself energetically by attuning with the Sun's light ahead of time.

It's ideal to spend some time by a river or other body of water, especially if it's a sunny day. Watch the sunrise and the sunset if you can. Many people like to stay up the whole night before in order to see the Sun rise on its most powerful day.

If the weather won't be fair on the solstice day itself, you can commune with Nature the day before or after. But if you're experiencing a string of rainy days, don't fret—the Sun is always there behind the clouds, and you can acknowledge that specifically in your ritual if you wish.

Covens located near a coastline may meet at the shore for their Litha celebrations, in honor of the balance between the Elements of Fire and Water. Rituals are ideally held outdoors, and groups may meet at sunrise on this day, or at "solar noon," the point in the day when the Sun is at its highest in the sky.

One common ritual acts out the story of the battle between the Oak King and the Holly King. In some Wiccan traditions, these twin aspects of the Sun God's annual journey take turns ruling the year. The Oak King, representing the light half of the year, reigns until the Summer Solstice, when he is cut down by the Holly King, who heralds in the beginning of the waning of the light. The ritual enactment serves as a reminder that there can be no light without the dark—it is the contrast between the two that makes each possible.

Magic is, of course, always an appropriate part of Sabbat celebrations, but at Litha the energies available from the abundant natural world are particularly potent. Plug into these currents with spellwork of your choosing. You may want to focus on goals related to love, beauty, friendship, healing, empowerment, or physical and magical energy, but all purposes are suitable at this time.

If you work with the faeries, be sure to acknowledge their presence with offerings of food and/or drink. The height of summer is a great time to watch the subtle movements of the trees in the wind. You just may see a faerie face or two—or even the Green Man himself—among the leaves. If you grow your own herbs, or know how to recognize them in the wild, make a point of gathering a few on this day to use in magical teas, charms, and other workings.

Making protective amulets is a popular magical tradition at this time. Wiccans and other Pagans tie a trio of protective herbs together with cloth to carry or wear around the neck for the coming year. The amulet is charged over the Midsummer bonfire (or a candle if need be). After the year is up, it is buried before a new one is made. Another type of amulet is made with the ashes of the Litha fire, carried in a pouch or kneaded into soft clay that is then baked in a kiln. Litha ashes also make great fertilizer for your garden!

Be sure to incorporate the Element of Fire into your magic, whether with a large ritual bonfire or a few simple candles. If it's a cloudy day, light a candle first thing in the morning and leave it to burn until sunset. This is a good time for clearing and charging crystals and other magical tools by leaving them in sunlight for a few hours. Divination related to love and romance is also traditional at this time, as are rituals of rededication to the God and Goddess.

LITHA CORRESPONDENCES

Colors: gold, green, red, orange, yellow, blue

Stones: emerald, amber, tiger's eye, jade

Herbs: St. John's wort, mugwort, vervain, mint, thyme, chamomile, parsley, oak and holly trees, lavender

Flowers: all flowers, but especially rose, honeysuckle, daisy, lily

Incense: pine, myrrh, rose, cedar, frankincense, lemon, sage, lavender

Altar decorations/symbols: roses, sunflowers, berries, oak and holly leaves, birds, butterflies, sea shells, pinwheels, yellow discs, other solar symbols and imagery

Foods: early summer fruits and vegetables, honey cakes, strawberries, fennel, lemon balm tea, red wine

SUMMER SOLSTICE COURAGE SPELL

With its long days of light and warmth, summer is a time for action and outward-focused energy. This is the perfect time of year to take on a project, enterprise or issue that you've been putting off due to fear of failure or fear of change. Whether you want to ask for a raise, learn to play a new instrument, go back to school, or get to the bottom of a problematic relationship, the energy of the Sun can help you tap into and strengthen your innate courage to dive into the task at hand.

At one point or another, everyone has some fear—whether conscious or unconscious—holding them back from achieving certain goals in life. The fiery essence of the Sun is both purifying and fortifying, allowing you to release your fears and strengthen your sense of well-being regardless of your circumstances.

This is the optimal state of mind from which to approach any kind of challenge, whether your aim is to solve a problem or to enrich your life with a new activity. The Sun card in the Tarot represents power, practicality, freedom and well-being. If you have a Tarot deck, pull out the Sun card and focus on its imagery in preparation for the spellwork.

This spell is suitable any time during the height of summer, but is extra powerful if worked on the day of the Solstice. For spectacular magic, gather your herbs on this day as well, whether you grow them in your garden or purchase them at the market. (You can also see if any of them grow near you in the wild!) Dried herbs will work fine, but in the spirit of lush summer abundance, strive for fresh if possible.

It's ideal to use all four of the herbs included in this spell, which are associated both with courage and with the magical energies of this Sabbat, but if this isn't possible, try to incorporate at least three.

You will need:

- 1 white work candle
- 1 orange spell or votive candle
- 1 teaspoon each of chopped fresh or dried lavender, vervain, St. John's wort and thyme
- Small bowl for mixing herbs
- Small heat-proof plat
- Sun Tarot card (optional)

Instructions:

Light the work candle.

Prop up the Sun card (if using) where you can see it while you work the spell.

Spend a few moments thinking about what it is you want to achieve and how you will feel when you've succeeded.

Hold this feeling in mind as you add the herbs to the bowl, one at a time, mixing them together with your fingertips.

Now hold the orange candle in both hands and charge it with your personal energy.

Visualize yourself outside in full sunlight, basking in the warmth and infused with bright light throughout your entire being. Send this light into the candle.

When you feel ready, place the candle (in a secure holder) on the plate.

Starting at the northernmost point, sprinkle the herbs in a clockwise circle around the base of the candle as you say the following (or similar) words:

> *"As the Sun shines bright at the height of its power,*
> *so my courage comes forth to light the way."*

Now, state your goal out loud as if you've already achieved it. (For example, "*I have enrolled in college classes to advance my career*" or "*I have embarked on a healthier eating plan.*")

Then light the candle and say "*So it is.*"

Leave the candle to burn out on its own.

You can sprinkle the herbs onto the Earth, or burn them in your cauldron.

LITHA ANOINTING OIL

This magical oil can be made at Litha and used year round to harness the powerful energies of the height of summer. Use natural essential oils rather than synthetic fragrance oils if at all possible.

You will need:

- Clean glass jar
- Brown glass bottle
- Small funnel
- 2 tablespoons sunflower oil
- 4 drops lavender oil
- 3 drops lemon oil
- 2 drops cinnamon oil
- 1 drop rose oil

Instructions:

Pour the sunflower oil into a clean glass jar.

Then add one essential oil at a time, taking a moment to inhale the aroma as you swirl the oils together in the jar, building a more and more complex scent as you go.

Funnel your newly-created blend into a brown glass bottle, seal tightly and let it sit outside in the shade for one hour.

If you clear and charge your crystals under the Litha Sun, try anointing them with the oil blend afterward and use them in charms and other spellwork.

LAMMAS

Northern Hemisphere: August 1 or 2

Southern Hemisphere: February 1 or 2

Pronounced: LAH-mahs

Themes: first fruits, harvest, gratitude, benevolent sacrifice, utilizing skills and talents

Also known as: Lughnasa, August Eve, Feast of Bread, Harvest Home, Gŵyl Awst, First Harvest

Situated on the opposite side of the Wheel from Imbolc, which heralds the end of the winter season, Lammas marks the beginning of the end of summer. It is the cross-quarter day between the Summer Solstice and the Autumn Equinox.

Although the days are still hot, sunshine is still abundant and the fields and forests are still teeming with life, we can begin to feel the telltale signs of the approaching autumn. The Sun sets earlier with each passing day, and many plants begin to wither, dropping their seeds to the ground so that new life can return at the start of the next growing season.

Berries, apples, and other fruits begin to ripen on trees and vines, and the grain in the fields has reached its full height, ready to be cut down and stored for the winter. This is a bittersweet time, as we are surrounded by the abundance of the summer's bounty, yet becoming more aware by the day that we are heading back into dark time of year.

Lammas is the time of the "first fruits" and is known in Wiccan and other Pagan traditions as the first of the three harvest festivals. Grain crops are now or soon will be ready for harvesting, along with corn and many other late-summer vegetables and early-autumn fruits. Of course, plenty of produce has already been available for harvesting, and plenty more will be ready later on in the season. But Lammas marks the point in time when harvesting, rather than planting or tending, becomes the main focus.

This is a time to consciously recognize the fruits of our labors—whether literally or metaphorically—and to give thanks for all that has manifested. We recognize the inherent sacrifice of the plants that give their lives so that we may eat, and we are humbled by the greater life-and-death cycles that govern all of creation.

Just six weeks after the Summer Solstice, the God at Lammas is now visibly on the wane. He is approaching his old age, rising later each morning and retiring sooner every night.

The Goddess in her Mother aspect is still waxing, as the Earth continues to bear the fruit of the seeds planted at the start of the growing season. She is still pregnant with the new God, who will be born at Yule, after the old God completes his journey to the Underworld at Samhain. This is one of the most poignant moments on the Wheel of the Year, as the Goddess demonstrates that life goes on even though we all experience loss and the fading of the light.

In ancient agricultural civilizations, grain was often associated with the death and rebirth cycle, and many Wiccan mythological traditions draw on this archetype at Lammas. In one version, the Sun God transfers his power to the living grain in the fields, and so is sacrificed when the grain is cut down. The God willingly sacrifices himself so that his people may live.

And yet the God is later reborn, ensuring that the crops will grow once again to feed the people for another year. The harvest practice of saving seed grain for planting next year's crop is both a practical necessity and a way of participating in the metaphor—saving the seeds is a way of ensuring the God's rebirth.

THE FIRST FRUITS

In the modern world, the first of August is not necessarily an important harvest date, and may seem quite early to some—after all, the summer is still in full swing! In fact, due to our advanced agricultural technology, there are now actually multiple growing cycles for various types of grain and other crops.

But back when harvesting, threshing, winnowing and sieving of the grain was all done by hand, farmers needed to start as early as they could. After all, once this hard work was done, it would be time to bring in the later-season crops ahead of the first killing frosts.

Of course, August 1st wasn't necessarily a hard and fast date for our ancestors, though it was considered the earliest acceptable time to begin bringing in the wheat. But if the crop wasn't quite ready, due to insufficient rain or sunshine, then the harvest—and the accompanying festivities—would wait. Nature's schedule was far more powerful than any calendar humans could devise.

Although the harvesting process meant long hours of hard work for the farmers, it was still cause for celebration and merriment. Many families' stores of wheat would have run very low or even empty by this time, and the onset of the harvest season meant that plenty of new abundance was on its way.

It was also a very social time, as neighbors worked together in order to bring the harvest in successfully for everyone in the community. Feasting was a must, and a special emphasis was placed on bread, as a staple of nourishment that would provide for the family throughout the long winter months and beyond.

The first loaves made from the first wheat of the new season were particularly significant, and in Anglo-Saxon England, these loaves were brought into the churches and laid on the altar to be blessed. This is where the holiday gets its name—the old Saxon phrase "hlaf-maesse," which translates literally to "loaf mass," and eventually became "Lammas."

The custom of blessing the bread makes Lammas an interesting example of how Christianity and pagan religions coexisted for a time. Bread is actually an important symbol in many spiritual traditions, going back to the ancient world.

For Wiccans and other modern Pagans, bread is representative of all the Elements: the seeds growing in the Earth, the yeast utilizing Water and Air to make the dough rise, and the Fire of the hearth making the finished product. Add to this the concept of Akasha—or Spirit—being present in the grain thanks to the power of the Sun, and you have a very sacred food indeed.

Given the significance of bread to the communion rituals of the Christian Church, it's easy to see how these traditions overlapped. But if the Church officials had hoped to stomp out pagan practices with the "loaf mass," they didn't succeed, at least not immediately—the Anglo-Saxon peasants were known to use their church-blessed bread in protection rituals and other magic.

As an agricultural festival, the First Harvest would certainly have preceded the arrival of Christianity to Europe. And yet it's unknown what this holiday was called in England prior to the custom that brought about the name of "Lammas." However, in Ireland the day was, and still is, known as Lughnasa (pronounced "LOO-na-sa" or "Loo-NOSS-ah," also spelled "Lughnasadh").

This cross-quarter festival was held as a tribute to the Celtic God Lugh, a warrior deity who was associated with the Sun, fire, grain, and many skills and talents such as smithcraft, building, music and magic. The association with grain comes from Lugh's foster mother, Tailtiu, who was said to have cleared the plains of Ireland for use in agriculture and died of exhaustion from doing so.

Lugh held an annual harvest festival in her honor, which included athletic games and contests that resembled the original Olympics, along with music and storytelling. This mythical festival was made real by the ancient Celts and was celebrated in one form or another well into the 20th century.

As with other ancient harvest festivals, Lughnasa was a time to offer the "first fruits" to the gods. The first of the crops were carried to the top of a high hill and buried there. Bilberries were gathered and a sacred bull was sacrificed for the great feast.

Ritual plays were performed in which Lugh defeated blight or famine and seized the harvest for the people. Dancing, drinking, trading and matchmaking were popular activities at the gatherings, which might last for three days before coming to a close. Handfastings and trial marriages (which lasted a year and a day and could then be broken or made permanent) were also common, as were visits to holy wells, where people would pray for good health and leave offerings of coins or strips of cloth.

CELEBRATING LAMMAS

Across the spectrum of Wiccan and other modern Pagan traditions, celebrations at Lammas can vary widely. Those inspired by the ancient Celts may choose to focus on honoring Lugh, and many call this holiday Lughnasa rather than Lammas. Others might be more rooted in Anglo-Saxon traditions, while still others incorporate a blend of ancient sources into their practice. Among all this diversity, however, the central theme is almost always the first harvest and the beginning of the transition into the darker, colder months.

Feasts are part of every Sabbat, but the significance of the feast is a particular focus during the harvest holidays, as we give thanks to the God and Goddess for the bounty of the Earth. Wiccans deliberately choose to prepare and savor the first "fruits" of the harvest season, whether it be apples and grapes, wheat and corn, or anything else that has come into season where they live. This feast is a physical participation in the turning of the Wheel of the Year, as we recognize that this time of newly-reaped abundance, like all other moments in time, will soon pass.

Coven rituals at Lammas often honor the waxing energy of the pregnant Goddess and the waning energy of the fading God. They give thanks for the manifestations of the year thus far, whether material, spiritual, or both. In some traditions, goals for the next two harvest Sabbats are stated, as well as intentions for the bounty of the Earth to be shared by all beings.

For solitary practitioners, a full-scale feast may be somewhat impractical, especially for those who live alone. If this is the case, you can still make a point of enjoying some fresh baked bread and late-summer fruits and vegetables as part of your Lammas celebration. Save any seeds from the fruits for planting, or use them in your spellwork.

Another way to mark this Sabbat is to make a corn dolly from corn stalks or straw. This is a manifestation of the ancient "Corn Mother" archetype found around the world. She can be placed on your altar and even used in magic. Since crafting is a way of honoring the Celtic god Lugh at this time, consider making and/or decorating other ritual items, such as a wand or pentacle.

You could also choose to practice any of your skills and talents, whether that means writing, playing an instrument, playing in a soccer or basketball game, or simply going for a nice long run. If there's a new skill you'd like to learn, now is a great time to get started.

Whatever you do, be sure to spend some time outdoors drinking in the sights, sounds, and smells of summer because they will be fading away before you know it!

LAMMAS CORRESPONDENCES

Colors: gold, yellow, orange, red, green, light brown
Stones: carnelian, citrine, peridot, aventurine, sardonyx

Herbs: sage, meadowsweet, ginseng, vervain, calendula, fenugreek, heather, dill, yarrow

Flowers: sunflower, passionflower, acacia flowers, cyclamen

Incense: sandalwood, frankincense, copal, rose, rose hips, rosemary, chamomile, passionflower

Altar decorations/symbols: first harvest fruits and vegetables, fresh baked bread, grapes and vines, corn dollies, sickles and scythes, Lugh's spear, symbols representing your own skills

Foods: apples, breads, all grains, berries, hazelnuts, summer squash, corn, elderberry wine, ale

LAMMAS GRATITUDE AND BREAD BLESSING RITUAL

As anyone who practices gratitude on a regular basis will tell you, it really pays to express appreciation for the blessings in your life. This is because of the Law of Attraction—the more you appreciate, the more you attract new things and circumstances to appreciate!

But it's also good to express gratitude simply for its own sake. Any Sabbat is an excellent occasion to do so, but it's especially appropriate at Lammas, the season of the first fruits.

This ritual provides a simple, elegant structure for thanking the God and Goddess, Nature, or whatever your term may be for the powers that govern the Universe. If seven candles are too much to manage for whatever reason, you can certainly use fewer, but it's nice to get a little decadent with this if you can.

You will need:

- 7 gold, yellow and orange candles (any size and in any combination)
- Handful of fresh sunflower and/or calendula petals
- Loaf of fresh-baked bread
- Pen (or pencil) and writing paper

Instructions:

Arrange the candles and sprinkle the petals among them in a manner that pleases you.

Place the bread in front of the candles and light one of them.

Now, make a list of at least 10 blessings you've experienced over the past few months. These can be hugely significant or "little things." Usually, it will be a combination of both. You will likely find that more and more things occur to you as you write (again, the Law of Attraction at work).

When you've got a good list together, light the rest of the candles and then read the list aloud, starting with "*Thank you for...*" before each item.

Now, hold the bread up toward the sky and say the following (or similar) words:

"God and Goddess, I thank you for this bread, which represents all the blessings I have listed here and more. May all on Earth be nourished by the bounty of Nature. So let it be."

Eat some of the bread, and be sure to use the rest of it over the coming days.

SKILL-BUILDING
CRYSTAL CHARM

In the spirit of Lugh, the god of many skills, this simple charm can support you in developing or strengthening any skill, whether it's related to work or leisure. You can use any crystal or mineral stone you feel an affinity with, but choosing one with Lammas/Lughnasa associations makes for a nice extra boost at this time of year.

Corresponding crystals include:

Aventurine: confidence, creativity, luck
Citrine: joy, success
Sardonyx: strength, willpower

You will need:

- 1 small-to-medium-sized crystal
- 1 red or yellow candle
- Rosemary, cinnamon, or other "activating" essential oil

Instructions:

Anoint the candle and the crystal with the oil.

Hold the crystal in your dominant hand and feel its energies moving through you.

Visualize yourself being highly proficient in your chosen skill.

Hold this feeling in your heart as you light the candle.

Place the crystal in front of the candle and allow the candle to burn out on its own.

Keep your crystal with you whenever you're practicing your skill, and rub it with your thumb whenever you need a little boost of confidence.

MABON
(AUTUMN EQUINOX)

Northern Hemisphere: September 21-24

Southern Hemisphere: March 20-22

Pronounced: MAY-bun, MAH-bun, MAY-vhon, or MAH-bawn

Themes: harvest, gratitude, abundance, balance, preparation, welcoming the dark

Also known as: Autumnal Equinox, Fall Equinox, September Equinox, Harvest Tide, Harvest Home, Harvest Festival, Wine Harvest, Feast of Avalon, Alben Elfed, Meán Fómhair, Gwyl canol Hydref

   Mabon is the name used by Wiccans and many other modern Pagans for the Sabbat falling at the Autumn Equinox. Compared to the solstices, which actually occur during the middle of their respective seasons, the equinoxes mark more significant shifts from one season to the next.

   By this point on the Wheel, the end of summer has become undeniable—a crisp chill in the air descends each evening at sunset, and the leaves on deciduous trees have begun to turn deep, bright shades of red, yellow and orange. The blue of the afternoon sky deepens as the summer's white-hot sunlight turns golden. Plant life dies back in gardens, fields and forests, and squirrels get busy gathering acorns and walnuts to stash away for the coming cold months.

For many people, this is a bittersweet moment, as the beauty of the transforming Earth reminds us that we're heading into bleak and barren times. But this is the true essence of the seasons and the Wheel—all of creation is always in motion, and the only constant in life is change.

The cyclical nature of time is especially apparent at Mabon as we work with themes that echo both Lammas and Ostara. Mabon is the second of the three harvest festivals, representing the pinnacle of abundance when it comes to the crops of the fields and the bounty of our gardens. Once again, we take time to appreciate all we have manifested—material and otherwise—through our efforts over the past several months.

There is more to do between now and Samhain to prepare for the winter, and this is a good time to take stock and evaluate what plans and projects need to be brought to completion before we enter the dark half of the year. But it's also a moment to pause and celebrate what has taken place thus far.

In doing so, we give thanks to those who have assisted us, whether they be friends, family, or spirit guides and ancestors on the other side. And we recognize the importance of sharing our good fortune with others, by hosting feasts as well as giving to those in need.

The other central focus at this time is balance. Like Ostara, which falls on the Spring Equinox, Mabon marks the point at which day and night are of equal length. This time, the Sun crosses the "celestial equator" and appears to head south. From now until Yule, the light will wane significantly, with the nights becoming noticeably longer than the days. However, at this moment, the light and the dark are balanced.

Interestingly, the Autumn Equinox coincides with the Sun's entrance into the Zodiac sign of Libra. Libra's symbol is the scales, and it is the sign known for seeking balance, harmony and equality. However much some of us may prefer warmth to cold or light to dark (or vice versa), we also know that without their opposites, we couldn't truly appreciate our favorite times of year. Participating in the turning of the Wheel through ritual and celebration helps us live in harmony with these shifting tides.

This recognition of the necessity of change—more specifically, the necessity of death in the life/death/rebirth cycle—is seen in the shifting relationship between the Goddess and the God. At Mabon, neither is young anymore.

The aging God is even further weakened than at Lammas, and will soon give way completely to the dominance of the dark at Samhain. The Goddess is still in her Mother aspect as the Earth continues to bear fruit, and she still holds the new God in her womb. Yet she is moving toward her Crone aspect as well, where she will reign alone over the dark, mysterious nights until the God is reborn at Yule.

The bittersweet quality of this time of year is embodied by the Goddess herself, who mourns the passing of the God yet knows he will return anew. In some traditions, the Goddess actually follows the God to the Underworld, which is why the Earth becomes cold and barren. In others, it is her sadness at his absence that causes the leaves to fall, the plants to die, and the animals to slumber away in hidden shelters. Still others view the coming weeks simply as a time of needed rest for all of the

Earth, the equal and balanced opposite of the active energy of spring.

THE HORN OF PLENTY

While the Autumn Equinox was celebrated in several places throughout Asia, there's little evidence to suggest that the ancient pagans of Europe marked this specific day with any major fanfare. However, harvest festivals were widely observed at some point during the fall season in many cultures.

In the areas comprising what is now the United Kingdom, the traditional harvest festival was tied to both the solar and lunar calendars, being held around the Full Moon closest to the Autumn Equinox. And the remains of ancient neolithic sites throughout Britain and Ireland which were designed to align with the Sun on this day show that it was considered an important moment to observe and honor.

This lack of historical information made the Autumn Equinox somewhat difficult to give a unique name to, at least compared to the other solar Sabbats. In the early 1970s, the name "Mabon" was suggested by Aidan Kelly, a prominent member of the growing Pagan community in the U.S.

Mabon is the name of a Welsh mythological figure who is mentioned in Arthurian legends. He is considered a deity by some, but not enough is known about him to confirm this status, as many figures in ancient pagan myths are the children of unions between deities and humans. Nonetheless, Mabon is the son of the goddess Modron, who is often described as the primordial triple goddess of the ancient Celts. The story we have of Mabon is that he was abducted from his mother when he was three days old, and held imprisoned in a secret location into adulthood, until he is rescued by King Arthur's men.

In actuality, "Mabon" means "son," and "Modron" means "mother," so we don't really know whether these two mythical figures had specific names. Yet these archetypes are somewhat fitting for a Wiccan Sabbat in that they echo the mother-child relationship of the God and Goddess.

As the mythology and symbolism of the Wheel of the Year has evolved, the tale of Mabon has grown into something new, with various writers borrowing elements of ancient myths from other cultures, especially the Greeks and the Norse. In one version, Modron's grief over her missing son is given as the reason for the turning of the season—her sadness causes darkness and cold to envelop the Earth. In another, it is Mabon's imprisonment deep within the ground that leads to the turning inward of animals and plant life.

As with Ostara, we can see that the lore around Mabon is rather more modern than that of most other Sabbats. Nonetheless, the sorrow inherent to the original tale can be seen as appropriate for this time of year, as the absence of light looms closer and closer.

If Ostara's symbols are the hare and the egg, then the chief symbol of Mabon is the cornucopia, also known as "the horn of plenty." This image—a large, hollowed-out horn filled to overflowing with fruits and vegetables—is widely recognized in North America as part of the modern "harvest festival" of Thanksgiving. However, it was part of the harvest festivals of Europe for many centuries before making its way to the new world.

The word "cornucopia" comes from the Latin words for "horn" and "plenty," but the symbol itself goes back even further to the ancient Greeks. It features prominently in Greek mythology, particularly in a story about Zeus as an infant. His supernatural strength caused him to accidentally break off one of the horns of Amalthea, the goat who watched over him and fed him with her milk. The severed horn then gained the power to provide infinite nourishment.

Other deities associated with the cornucopia include the Greek goddesses Gaia (the Earth) and Demeter (a grain goddess) and the Roman goddess Abundantia (the personification of abundance). As we can see, the cornucopia is a very fitting symbol for this Wiccan Sabbat—not just because of its pagan origins, but also because of its association with the Horned God.

CELEBRATING MABON

The cornucopia is an excellent place to start when it comes to your own Mabon celebration. You can make your own completely from scratch or buy a horn-shaped basket and fill it with fresh autumn produce, nuts, herbs, flowers and even crystals to place on your altar.

Use it in ritual to express gratitude for the abundance in your life, and/or in spellwork for abundance and prosperity. You can also leave it outdoors at night as an offering to the animals and faeries, and bury whatever isn't eaten by the end of the following day. The cornucopia also makes an excellent gift and a way for you to share the bounty in your life with others.

Coven rituals at Mabon often focus on balance and on giving thanks for life's blessings, particularly those that have come to pass over the past several months. New or continuing goals may be identified for the next and final harvest at Samhain. The

Mabon feast is particularly lavish as we are at the height of the harvest season. Food is often shared with shelters and other organizations on behalf of the less fortunate.

There is also an acknowledgment of the coming dark, with thanks given to the retreating Sun. In some traditions, it is time to actively welcome the dark, and to honor spirits and aging deities—especially Crone goddesses—in preparation for Samhain.

For Witches who tend gardens, now is the time to harvest what is ready, tend what is still growing, and collect and save seeds for next year's crops. You might make an offering to nature spirits with some of your bounty, or offer seeds, grains and acorns or cider.

Be sure to spend quality time outdoors, drinking in the last of the sunshine. Gather brightly colored leaves to place on your altar, and give thanks to the Goddess and God for the graceful beauty with which they bring the light half of the year to a close. For spellwork, consider goals related to harmony and balance, as well as protection, prosperity, and self-confidence.

MABON CORRESPONDENCES

Colors: deep reds, maroon, orange, yellow, gold, bronze, brown

Stones: amber, topaz, citrine, tiger's eye, lapis lazuli, sapphire, yellow agate

Herbs: chamomile, milkweed, thistle, yarrow, saffron, hops, Solomon's seal, sage, rue, hazel, ivy, oakmoss, mace

Flowers: marigold, sunflower, rose, aster, chrysanthemum

Incense: benzoin, cedar, pine, myrrh, frankincense, sandalwood, cinnamon, clove, sage

Altar decorations/symbols: cornucopia, gourds, acorns, pine cones, pinwheels, yellow discs, other solar symbols and imagery

Foods: nuts, wheat and other grains, bread, grapes, apples, pumpkin, pomegranate, all autumn fruits and vegetables, wine

MABON
FLOATING CANDLE SPELL

Mabon, like its "twin" Ostara, is a time to reflect on harmony and balance. But whereas the Spring Equinox is focused on balance in your relationship with the outer world, the Autumn Equinox asks you to turn your focus inward.

What aspects of your relationship with yourself could use some balancing? Are you open and listening to your own inner guidance, or are you letting the opinions of others get in the way? Are you speaking kindly to and about yourself or are you always being your own harshest critic? What nagging thoughts or emotions might you be in the habit of ignoring or stuffing down?

Traditionally, Autumn is associated with the Element of Water, which rules the psychic and emotional tides that ebb and flow between our conscious and unconscious selves. This spell makes use of the theme of balance with a candle floating in a cauldron. Use it as a portal to strengthen your inner balance for the coming season, and as a way of preparing for any shadow work you'd like to take on at Samhain.

You will need:

- 1 work candle
- 1 white floating candle
- Small cauldron or bowl
- Marigold or sunflower petals

Instructions:

Light the work candle.

Fill the cauldron with water up to about 1/2 inch from the top.

Sprinkle the flower petals on the water's surface, and gently float the candle among the petals.

Spend some time journaling about any inner conflicts or questions you'd like to harmonize within yourself. Try to write for at least 20 minutes.

When you feel you've hit on a particular aspect of yourself that could use some balancing at this time, write a short phrase or draw a symbol that represents it.

Light the floating candle as you keep this phrase or symbol in your third eye.

Sit quietly for a few moments and take in the sight of the flame, the water, and the petals.

You may wish to resume writing and/or stay open for any insights that come to you regarding your issue.

Leave the candle to burn out on its own.

AUTUMN PROTECTION CHARM

This charm can be used at any time of year, but it's especially appropriate for the autumn season when the impending darkness can start to get slightly under your skin.

Keep negativity at bay with a combination of herbs and minerals from the Earth. Each of the stones and herbs below are used in protection magic. Select those that resonate with you most for a personalized charm. For optimal protective powers, use at least two of the three herbs listed below.

You will need:

- Small drawstring bag
- 1-2 pieces of tiger's eye, amber, and/or carnelian
- 1 tablespoon each of sage, chamomile, and/or yarrow

Instructions:

Charge your ingredients in direct sunlight for one hour.

As you place them in the drawstring bag, visualize yourself surrounded by golden light.

Carry the charm with you whenever you feel highly energetically sensitive.

SAMHAIN

Northern Hemisphere: October 31 or November 1

Southern Hemisphere: April 30 or May 1

Pronounced: SOW-in, SAH-vin, or SOW-een

Themes: death, rebirth, divination, honoring ancestors, introspection, benign mischief, revelry

Also known as: Samhuin, Oidhche Shamhna, Halloween, Third Harvest, Day of the Dead, Feast of the Dead (Félie Na Marbh), Shadowfest, Ancestor Night, Feile Moingfinne (Snow Goddess), Winter Nights, Old Hallowmas, Calan Gaeaf

Of all the Sabbats, Samhain is considered to be the most powerful and important to Wiccans and other Witches, with many intense energies at play. This is when we honor the Death element of the life/death/rebirth cycle that forms the basis of the Wheel of the Year and all of Nature as we know it.

Wiccans understand that the death stage of the cycle is actually the most potent, as it is here that all potential for new life resides, waiting to be manifested into specific form.

Therefore, Samhain is the most fitting time for reflecting on our lives, looking back over the past year and identifying any circumstances or patterns of behavior we would like to allow to die, in order to make room for the new when the growing season begins again. By letting go of our old selves, we can move into the winter months ahead with clarity and acceptance of the ever-turning wheel of life and death.

The name "Samhain" has been translated from the Old Irish as "summer's end," and this date marked the beginning of the dark half of the year in the ancient Celtic world. This is the third and final harvest festival, the time to stock the root cellars with the last of the winter squashes, turnips, beets and other root vegetables, and to dry the last of the magical and medicinal herbs for winter storage.

The fields are now empty of their crops, the once-green meadow grasses are dying back to gold and brown, and the leaves have peaked and fallen, leaving the trees bare and stark against the greying skies. The chill in the air that began with Mabon is now here to stay, and the weakened Sun gives barely a passing glance for a few short hours before descending again below the horizon.

Indeed, it can seem as if the world is dying at this time. But this feeling is alleviated by the gratitude we express for all the abundance of the past year, and the knowledge that the light will return again, as is promised by the Wheel.

The perpetual life/death/rebirth cycle is characterized by both the God and the Goddess at Samhain.

In his Sun aspect, the God has aged considerably since Mabon. His power is nearly gone, and he descends into the Underworld, leaving the Earth to the darkness of winter. As the Horned God, or the God of the Hunt, he is a fully matured stag who gives his life so his people can survive the coming barren season. Wiccans say farewell to the God at this Sabbat, thanking him for fulfilling his life-sustaining roles over the past year and expressing faith that he will return, reborn, at Yule.

In many traditions, the Goddess is said to be mourning the God at this time, yet she too knows that he will return, as she is now in her wise Crone aspect. From the aged Crone we learn that death is part of life, that the old must be released in order for us to learn, grow, and birth new manifestations.

It is interesting that the Goddess herself never dies, since the Earth remains steadily present throughout the year, no matter where the Sun may be. Yet she represents death and life simultaneously—she is both Crone and mother-to-be of the new God.

SPIRITS AND SYMBOLS

For the Celts, from whom the name and many customs of this Sabbat are borrowed, Samhain was something of a dark mirror to Beltane—a counterpart of sorts which sits directly opposite the Wheel.

Once again, it was time to move the cattle, only now they were brought back to their winter pastures. The ritual bonfires and great gatherings that celebrated fertility in May were now a recognition of the abundance manifested throughout the light half of the year.

This was the time to gather the last harvest of the apples and nuts, and to select the animals that would be slaughtered to feed the people for the coming months. The meat would be salted and stored for the winter, and the bones from the Samhain feast were thrown upon the fires as offerings to secure good fortune for the next season's cattle. (This tradition gives us the word "bonfire"—"bone + fire.")

The gatherings at Samhain were festive affairs, as people danced, drank, feasted, and traded goods for the last time before winter kept everyone close to home. It was clearly an important time, as many key tales in early Irish mythology occur at Samhain.

As the first day of winter and the beginning of the dark half of the year, Samhain was, like its Beltane counterpart, a time of open passageways between the world of the living and the Otherworld, or world of the spirit. However, whereas Beltane focused on summer and the bursting forth of life that warmth and sunshine bring, Samhain was an acknowledgment of the cold, the dying back of the Earth, and the dead themselves who have gone before us.

Samhain Eve was, like Beltane Eve, a time of heightened activity on the part of the Aos Sí, or faeries, who were said to be extra mischievous now. These supernatural beings were to be steered clear of, to the extent that people avoided being out of doors on this night. If they had to leave home, they would carry iron or salt to discourage the Aos Sí from coming near. It was also believed that the Aos Sí needed to be appeased in order to ensure that the family and its livestock survived the coming winter, so offerings of food and drink were left for the faeries outside the door of the house.

With the Otherworld so easily accessible, Samhain was also a time for honoring the dead, who were thought to wander about and visit their family homes, seeking a warm welcome and a meal. The Samhain feast always included a place at the table reserved for the ancestors, and room was also left for them by the hearth. To make sure their loved ones could find

115

their way, a single candle was lit in each window of the house. People also left apples along the roadsides for spirits who had no living relatives to welcome them.

In general, it was believed that the dead, like the Aos Sí, had to be appeased at this time or misfortune might fall upon the family. However, blessings could be bestowed by appreciative departed souls as well. This belief in the need to placate the dead is found in ancient cultures around the world, and is seen most explicitly today in the Mexican Day of the Dead, which begins on October 31 and has roots in both European and Aztec cultures.

Since the spirit world was so readily accessible at Samhain, divination was a popular activity during the festival. Many different forms were practiced, often to discover information about future marriages or deaths. People's names were marked on stones which were then thrown into the bonfire. These would be plucked from the ashes the next day and "read" according to the condition they were in.

Crows and other birds were counted as they passed in the sky, with their number or direction being assigned specific meanings. Apples and nuts were often used in divination games. One popular activity was peeling an apple in one unbroken strip, casting the peel onto the floor, and reading the shape to find the first letter of the name of one's future spouse.

Another tradition evolved into what we now know as "bobbing for apples." In Celtic mythology, the apple was associated with immortality and the Otherworld. Hazelnuts were associated with divine wisdom, and were chewed by Druids in Scottish myths in order to gain prophecies.

There are many aspects of our modern Halloween celebrations that have their roots in Samhain customs. The fear of faeries and spirits roaming the night led our Celtic ancestors to disguise themselves in white, as if to blend in with the ghosts, or wear costumes made of straw to confuse them. This evolved into the tradition of "guising," in which people dressed in disguise to represent the spirits of the night and travelled from house to house collecting gifts of apples, nuts and other food for the Samhain feast.

In Scotland in particular, it was common for those imitating the mischievous faeries to play pranks on their neighbors, especially if they did not receive an offering from the household. These original "trick-or-treaters" carried lanterns made from hollowed-out turnips, which were often carved with frightening faces to either represent or ward off evil spirits. The lanterns were also left on windowsills or doorsteps to protect the home on Samhain Eve, a custom which later evolved into our modern "jack-o-lanterns."

Other symbols of Halloween which may have originated with the Celts include the skull and the skeleton. The skull was revered by Celtic warriors as the house of the soul and the seat of one's power, and it is thought that skulls were used as oracles. Skeleton imagery, seen particularly in Day of the Dead celebrations, is traced by some back to ancient Europe.

A classic symbol of Halloween is, of course, the Witch and all of her associated imagery—the broom, the cauldron and the black cat. Of course, this link stems from the misguided fear of "evil witches" promoted by the Christian Church in later centuries, but nonetheless it can be attributed to the connection that these shamanic practitioners had to the world of spirit.

There's a nice bit of irony here, in that Samhain—the "Witch's holiday"— seems to be the one that the Church just couldn't stamp out. For although November 1 was converted to

"All Saints' Day," the old pagan trappings of the original festival remain alive and well, even in mainstream culture.

CELEBRATING SAMHAIN

For Wiccans and other Pagans, Samhain is very much rooted in the ancient Celtic traditions. It is often described as the night when "the veil between the worlds is at its thinnest," and many choose to honor their ancestors and other departed loved ones at this time. Food and drink are left out for any wandering spirits, and many Witches seek communication with the Other Side.

We do not fear mischief or retribution from the dead, as we know our ancestors don't mean us harm, but we do honor and respect their presence. The Wiccan belief in reincarnation is also meditated upon at Samhain, as we recognize that the life/death/rebirth cycle applies to all living beings. We know that we do not return to the Other Side permanently, but rest and enjoy ourselves there until we're ready to be reborn into the physical world.

Samhain is a key occasion for divination of all kinds, including scrying, Tarot, runes and I-Ching, as well as various uses of apples. For those who work with the faeries, this is definitely an important night to leave offerings for them!

In many traditions, Samhain is also considered the start of the new year, as it is believed that the Celtic year began on the evening of October 31st. Scholars disagree about whether there is sufficient evidence for this, but Samhain is listed in Irish medieval literature as the first of the four cross-quarter day festivals, so the association has stuck.

Whether your tradition considers the year to begin now or at Yule, however, Samhain is an excellent time to reflect on your life and any changes you wish to make during the year ahead. This is the time in between death and new life, as the Crone/Mother Goddess waits for the God to be reborn.

What in your personal world do you wish to allow to die, and what new developments would you like to give birth to? What has ended that you need to fully let go of in order to make room for the new?

Coven rituals at Samhain are often held outdoors, at night, around a sacred bonfire. The coven members may focus on letting go of bad habits and other unwanted energies, symbolically releasing them into the fire to be transformed. Other ritual themes may include bidding farewell to the Old God, tapping into the wisdom of the Crone, and formally honoring the dead.

And of course, any Wiccans who practice spellwork are certain to do so on this night, the most potent time of the entire year for magic! Any type of work is bound to be effective, but in keeping with the themes of this Sabbat, goals related to banishing, releasing, and strengthening your psychic abilities are especially appropriate.

On your Samhain altar, include photographs or mementos from deceased loved ones and light a votive candle specifically for them. Since this is the Sabbat most associated with Witchcraft, include symbols like cauldrons, besoms (ritual brooms), and pentacles, even if you don't necessarily work with these tools regularly. As always, seasonal decorations of all kinds are key, but try to include a pumpkin if you can—carved and illuminated if possible!

Finally, be sure to give your sacred space a very thorough sweeping before beginning any ritual or spellwork. As you clean, visualize all unwanted energies and influences from the past year being swept away and out of your life.

SAMHAIN CORRESPONDENCES

<u>Colors:</u> black, orange, rust, bronze, brown, grey, silver, gold

<u>Stones:</u> jet, obsidian, onyx, smoky quartz, all other black stones, bloodstone, carnelian

<u>Herbs:</u> mugwort, wormwood, valerian, rosemary, sage, catnip, broom, oak leaves, witch hazel, angelica, deadly nightshade*, mandrake*,

<u>Flowers:</u> marigold, chrysanthemums, sunflower, goldenrod, Russian sage, pansies

<u>Incense:</u> nutmeg, mint, sage, copal, myrrh, clove, heather, heliotrope, benzoin, sweetgrass, sandalwood

<u>Altar decorations/symbols:</u> oak leaves and other fallen leaves, pomegranates, pumpkins, squashes, gourds, photos or other tokens of deceased loved ones, acorns, Indian corn, besom, cauldron

<u>Foods:</u> pumpkins, pomegranates, apples, all root vegetables and autumn/winter squashes, all nuts, breads, beans, apple cider, mulled cider, ale, herbal teas

*These herbs are highly toxic and should be used with care in spellwork only. Do not ingest!

SPELL TO END A BAD HABIT

With its emphasis on banishing and the death of the old, Samhain is a perfect opportunity to get some magical assistance with releasing any habit you want to be free of. The only caveat is that you have to *want* to end the habit. Without that motivation, this spell is unlikely to succeed.

You will need:

- 1 work candle (optional)
- 1 black candle
- 5 pieces of jet, obsidian, onyx, smokey quartz, and/or black tourmaline
- Small square of paper
- Pen or pencil (or ink and quill)
- Cauldron or other heat-proof dish

Instructions:

Light the work candle, if using.

Arrange the stones around the cauldron in a pentagram shape.

Light the black candle and sit quietly, imagining the freedom and vitality you will experience with this habit gone from your life.

When you're ready, write the habit on the square of paper.

Holding it in your dominant hand, raise it over the candle flame and say the following (or similar) words:

> *"As the fire burns among these stones*
> *I ask the blessings of the Crone:*
> *Release this habit written here*
> *without judgement, without fear."*

Now ignite the paper with the flame. (Be careful not to burn your fingers!)

When it's burning enough to incinerate completely, drop it into the cauldron.

Take the ashes outside and sprinkle them onto the Earth.

Allow the candle to burn out on its own.

Bury the stones or throw them in a creek or river to cast away all remaining traces of the habit.

SPIRIT-GUIDED WRITING

Automatic writing is a very effective way to channel insights and advice from the spirit realm. Each of us has guides on the Other Side with wisdom to share if we only tap into their energies.

If you write in a journal regularly, you have most likely already received information from the spirit world, in the form of inspired thoughts that seem to flow out of the pen without effort. Automatic writing is similar, only you're deliberately asking for the words to come through you, without your conscious mind making any decisions about the content or otherwise interfering in the process.

If writing at your altar isn't practical, transform a desk or table into your sacred space for this work. Be sure to ground and center yourself by meditating, taking a ritual bath, or any other activity that helps you connect with your own highest energy.

Opening yourself up to spirit energy can be disorienting and even unpleasant if you're not properly grounded, so it's especially important to prepare yourself energetically before you begin.

You will need:

- 1 white candle
- Mugwort
- Sage bundle
- Quartz crystal
- Amethyst
- Journal or sheets of paper
- Pen or pencil

<u>Instructions:</u>

Light the candle, and place the quartz and amethyst on either side of it.

Use the flame to ignite the sage, and smudge yourself and your surroundings to clear away any unwanted energy.

Take a few deep breaths and say the following (or similar) words:

> *"I surround myself in love and light*
> *and seek my spirits' guidance tonight.*
> *Guardians wise and helpers sage,*
> *Speak truth to me through pen and page."*

To prime the psychic connection between you and your guides, gently rub mugwort over the front and back of your journal (or on the first and last sheets of paper).

Then take up your pen (or pencil) and begin writing whatever comes to mind.

It may take a little while before your conscious mind lets go and the words begin to feel that they're coming from outside of you. If you like, you can write down a question to get started, but don't be surprised if what comes through is on a different topic altogether—you're asking for what the Universe most wants you to know at this time.

Write for at least 10 to 15 minutes. Remember, don't pay conscious attention to what you're writing—instead, let your eyes focus softly on your hand, your pen, or the candle as you let the automatic writing take over.

When you're ready to stop, set the pen down, shake out both of your hands, and then read what you've written.

You may want to save the pages and return to them a few weeks or months down the road, to see how the messages fit with your life as it's unfolding.

CONCLUSION

Ideally, no matter what form your individual spiritual practice takes, the act of honoring and celebrating the Wheel of the Year should be viewed as an art, rather than a rigid, unchanging routine.

A dynamic, creative and evolving approach to connecting with Nature and the divine is at the heart of Wicca and other modern branches of Paganism. This guide was written in that spirit, offering insight and information that will hopefully help you to build your own unique relationship with the Wheel of the Year.

As you progress along your path from one season to the next, the Sabbats provide regular opportunities to learn and grow in your faith. And as the years go by, the experience of "turning the Wheel" becomes richer and more rewarding. Indeed, the wise among us say that you are never done learning, so by all means don't stop your Sabbat education at the end of this guide.

As a next step in expanding your knowledge, you might check out some of the resources listed on the following page. And no matter where you go from here, may the God and Goddess be ever present with you on your path.

Blessed Be.

SUGGESTIONS FOR FURTHER READING

The Wheel of the Year is truly an enormous topic, with so many variations among traditions and individuals who celebrate the Sabbats.

While you'll no doubt find some similar information in many other resources, each author has their own individual experiences and perspective on these days of power. As with anything else in Wicca or the larger Pagan world, it's always worth the effort to learn as much as you can in order to deepen your own practice.

This brief list of books offers some solid places to start. Happy reading!

Pauline Campanelli, *Wheel of the Year: Living the Magical Life* (1989)

Eileen Holland, *The Spellcaster's Reference: Magickal Timing for the Wheel of the Year* (2009)

Edain McCoy, *Sabbats: A Witch's Approach to Living the Old Ways* (2002)

Judy Ann Nock, *The Provenance Press Guide to the Wiccan Year: A Year Round Guide to Spells, Rituals, and Holiday Celebrations* (2007)

Nigel Pennick, *The Pagan Book of Days: A Guide to the Festivals, Traditions, and Sacred Days of the Year* (2009)

FREE AUDIOBOOK PROMOTION

Don't forget, you can now enjoy a free audiobook version of any of my books when you start a free 30-day trial with Audible. This includes best-sellers such as *Wicca for Beginners* and *Wicca Book of Spells*.

Members receive free audiobooks every month, as well as exclusive discounts. And, if you don't want to continue with Audible, just remember to cancel your membership. You won't be charged a cent, and you'll get to keep your book!

To download this or any of my 20+ books on Wicca and related topics, simply visit:

www.wiccaliving.com/free-audiobook

Happy listening!

MORE BOOKS BY LISA CHAMBERLAIN

Wicca for Beginners: A Guide to Wiccan Beliefs, Rituals, Magic, and Witchcraft

Wicca Book of Spells: A Book of Shadows for Wiccans, Witches, and Other Practitioners of Magic

Wicca Herbal Magic: A Beginner's Guide to Practicing Wiccan Herbal Magic, with Simple Herb Spells

Wicca Book of Herbal Spells: A Book of Shadows for Wiccans, Witches, and Other Practitioners of Herbal Magic

Wicca Candle Magic: A Beginner's Guide to Practicing Wiccan Candle Magic, with Simple Candle Spells

Wicca Book of Candle Spells: A Book of Shadows for Wiccans, Witches, and Other Practitioners of Candle Magic

Wicca Crystal Magic: A Beginner's Guide to Practicing Wiccan Crystal Magic, with Simple Crystal Spells

Wicca Book of Crystal Spells: A Book of Shadows for Wiccans, Witches, and Other Practitioners of Crystal Magic

Tarot for Beginners: A Guide to Psychic Tarot Reading, Real Tarot Card Meanings, and Simple Tarot Spreads

Runes for Beginners: A Guide to Reading Runes in Divination, Rune Magic, and the Meaning of the Elder Futhark Runes

Wicca Moon Magic: A Wiccan's Guide and Grimoire for Working Magic with Lunar Energies

Wicca Wheel of the Year Magic: A Beginner's Guide to the Sabbats, with History, Symbolism, Celebration Ideas, and Dedicated Sabbat Spells

Wicca Kitchen Witchery: A Beginner's Guide to Magical Cooking, with Simple Spells and Recipes

Wicca Essential Oils Magic: A Beginner's Guide to Working with Magical Oils, with Simple Recipes and Spells

Wicca Elemental Magic: A Guide to the Elements, Witchcraft, and Magical Spells

Wicca Magical Deities: A Guide to the Wiccan God and Goddess, and Choosing a Deity to Work Magic With

Wicca Living a Magical Life: A Guide to Initiation and Navigating Your Journey in the Craft

Magic and the Law of Attraction: A Witch's Guide to the Magic of Intention, Raising Your Frequency, and Building Your Reality

Wicca Altar and Tools: A Beginner's Guide to Wiccan Altars, Tools for Spellwork, and Casting the Circle

Wicca Finding Your Path: A Beginner's Guide to Wiccan Traditions, Solitary Practitioners, Eclectic Witches, Covens, and Circles

Wicca Book of Shadows: A Beginner's Guide to Keeping Your Own Book of Shadows and the History of Grimoires

Modern Witchcraft and Magic for Beginners: A Guide to Traditional and Contemporary Paths, with Magical Techniques for the Beginner Witch

FREE GIFT REMINDER

As a thank-you gift to my readers, you can also download a free eBook version of *Wicca: Little Book of Spells.* These ten spells are ideal for newcomers to the practice of magic, but are also suitable for any level of experience!

You can download it by visiting:

www.wiccaliving.com/bonus

I hope you enjoy it!

DID YOU ENJOY *WICCA WHEEL OF THE YEAR MAGIC*?

Thanks so much for reading this book! I know there are many great books out there about Wicca, so I really appreciate you choosing this one.

If you enjoyed the book, I have a small favor to ask—would you take a couple of minutes to leave a review for this book on Amazon?

Your feedback will help me to make improvements to this book, and to create even better ones in the future. It will also help me develop new ideas for books on other topics that might be of interest to you. Thanks in advance for your help!

Made in the USA
Monee, IL
05 March 2020